The Self-Esteem REgime

The Self-Esteem REgime

*An Action Plan for Becoming
the Confident Person You Were Meant to Be*

Clarissa Burt
with
Gary M. Krebs
Foreword by Sharon Lechter

ROWMAN & LITTLEFIELD
Lanham • Boulder • New York • London

Published by Rowman & Littlefield
An imprint of The Rowman & Littlefield Publishing Group, Inc.
4501 Forbes Boulevard, Suite 200, Lanham, Maryland 20706
www.rowman.com

86-90 Paul Street, London EC2A 4NE, United Kingdom

Distributed by NATIONAL BOOK NETWORK

British Library Cataloguing in Publication Information Available

Library of Congress Cataloging-in-Publication Data

Names: Burt, Clarissa, author. | Krebs, Gary M., author.
Title: The self-esteem regime : an action plan for becoming the confident person
    you were meant to be / Clarissa Burt, with Gary M. Krebs.
Description: Lanham : Rowman & Littlefield, [2021] | Includes bibliographical
    references and index. | Summary: "Despite years of progress, many women
    still suffer low self-esteem in various realms of life. Here, Clarissa Burt shares
    her program for building better self-esteem through a unique process that
    emphasizes awareness, poise, and assurance"—Provided by publisher.
Identifiers: LCCN 2021017385 (print) | LCCN 2021017386 (ebook) | ISBN
    9781538152690 (paperback ; alk. paper) | ISBN 9781538152706 (epub)
Subjects: LCSH: Self-esteem.
Classification: LCC BF697.5.S46 B777 2021 (print) | LCC BF697.5.S46
    (ebook) | DDC 158.1—dc23
LC record available at https://lccn.loc.gov/2021017385
LC ebook record available at https://lccn.loc.gov/2021017386

This book is dedicated to all of the people who never felt good enough and now, after reading this book, will get up, move on, and never look back.

A girl should be two things . . .
CLASSY and FABULOUS.

—Coco Chanel

~

Contents

~

Foreword

I'm proud to say I have been friends with Clarissa Burt for some time and have appeared on her fabulous and informative *In the Limelight* podcast. I can't think of anyone I know who is better suited to write *The Self-Esteem REgime*. Not only is she classy and talented, she understands the internal turmoil people go through when they suffer from lack of self-confidence.

Negativity circulates around us. It strikes us when we are at work, with our families, and even in our interactions with friends, neighbors, and total strangers. The news is a constant source of negativity with its philosophy of "If it bleeds, it leads." It takes a lot to stay positive when we are surrounded by depressing information so much of the time. It requires focus and a true commitment to change—as Clarissa lays out in this book—to counter all of this noise.

It is human nature to lament and lean toward the negative. I couldn't agree more with what Clarissa writes in chapter 4, "REplace," on the subject: "Negative words can inflict an enormous amount of harm on your psyche—especially when they are self-generated in your head. In a sense, your personal inner voice—which is really just noise—turns you into your worst enemy. I would bet many things you think or say aloud about yourself are far worse than anything said to you by people who were angry at you or simply didn't like you. . . . Self-harming internal language must *always* be replaced."

If you are someone who uses negative thought as a survival tactic, give yourself a break. Recognize that your brain may be hardwired to go straight to the downside as a reaction to any circumstance—a phenomenon known as *negative bias*. This does not have to be a permanent state. Once you recognize when negativity has overtaken your thinking, you can start to become positive by owning that you have the power to influence your thoughts and even replace them. If, however, you continue to remain locked in the negative cycle, life will seem to continuously mistreat you and the occurrence of "bad things" happening will become a self-fulfilling prophecy.

For instance, I happen to be a worrier. In fact, I would say I am a champion of worry. A few years ago, I found an explanation of worry that said: "To worry is to pray for what you *do not* want." This simple definition has had a profound impact on my life. When you worry, you focus on a negative outcome and therefore attract negativity. Now when I find myself starting to worry about something, I stop and reframe my thoughts from what I *don't* want to happen into what I *do* want to happen. The results of reframing your thoughts from negativity to positivity are magical. By sharing this definition with people around the world, I have seen others change their lives for the positive as well.

When you want to build muscle mass, you must train. When you want to learn a new skill, you must train. Improving your self-esteem is about *retraining*, which isn't all that different from these two things, which is why you must have *The Self-Esteem REgime* in your arsenal.

By reading this book you have already taken the first big step in your battle against low self-esteem and set forth on your journey toward achieving success and happiness. You now have Clarissa Burt as an ally by your side, providing helpful tips, powerful encouragement, and supportive affirmations to help you defeat your inner demons. Consider her your personal coach, cheerleader, counselor, big sister, and best friend, all rolled into one beautiful package.

As your self-esteem increases, you will see others attracted to you naturally as a result of your new habits and attitude of positivity. You will become a beacon of light by standing in your power and, as a result, you will attract others who want to add their lights to yours. Thank you, Clarissa, for providing such a beautiful guide for all of us to chart a course for a more beautiful future.

I end every episode of my daily ATMs (Abundance, Tips, and Mentorship) by telling the listeners that they are *fabulous*. Please look in the mirror and tell yourself "I am *fabulous*!" And hear me saying, "Yes, you are!"

To your success!

—Sharon Lechter, author of *Think and Grow Rich for Women*, coauthor of *Exit Rich, Three Feet from Gold, Outwitting the Devil, Rich Dad Poor Dad*, and fourteen other books in the Rich Dad series

Acknowledgments

I'd like to acknowledge the millions of people all over the world who have been abandoned, abused, beaten, hit, struck, oppressed, depressed, distressed, held back, lied to, cheated on, lost, betrayed, deceived, misled, double-crossed, walked out on, stabbed in the back, sold down the river, stolen from, deserted, discarded, shunned, cast out, dropped, dumped, forgotten, neglected, rejected, and/or dejected. You are the sole reason I have written this book.

You are also inspiration for my every breath. This is not a book for me; it's a mission and a movement. My greatest wish is to see everyone in the world living as happy, healthy esteemed beings—free from hate, free from fear, free from abuse and despair.

Both Gary and I would like to extend our sincere thanks to everyone who helped us produce this book, particularly Suzanne Staszak-Silva and Deni Remsberg at Rowman & Littlefield. Additionally, we are grateful to Nora Gray, Brooke Walker, Mary L. Holden, Dr. Jeffrey Fannin, Didi Wong, and Ilana Krebs, as well as Margot, Tiffany, Debbie, Delicia, Pat, Lisa, Heidi, Selena, Kate, and Peter, whose names have been changed out of respect for their privacy.

INTRODUCTION

~

You Deserve to Look Good and Feel Good Right Now

Some books simply *have* to be written. I originally started out writing a book for me: to help me understand myself better. Shortly after jotting down some notes, I realized that I was writing a book for *you*. Whether you're a student, working mom, small business owner, corporate executive, salesperson, teacher, factory worker, engineer, artist, hairstylist, real estate agent, corporate executive, waitress, or anything else, this book is about something inside of you: an inner strength and power you've always had but that ended up buried deep inside your being.

No doubt you are someone who works hard, lives, and loves. You try to do it all and do it well, carrying all of the burdens for your family. Perhaps, along with managing your career and home life, you've been caring for an ill family member, such as a significant other, parent, or child. Or maybe you've been coping with your own physical ailments and emotional traumas, along with supporting everyone else's.

Readers like you are the exceptional people of today. You have accomplished many great things against all odds. You know full well the value of people and things, and yet the world has been on your shoulders and beaten you down so much for so long you're no longer sure of your own worth. Perhaps you've taken a few lumps over the years—from your family, your spouse or significant other, your job, or

1

your community. No wonder you aren't satisfied or happy with all of that constant pressure!

It occurs to you that you should feel proud of everything you've accomplished and what you do single every day. You *deserve* to look good, feel good, enjoy life, and be happy. And yet, inexplicably, you don't.

A moment comes. Maybe it's right after your divorce. Maybe your last child has moved away from home. Maybe you've recently had to place your parent in a retirement facility. Or maybe you're just in a rut at your job.

You look in the mirror. What do you see? Do you start to count the wrinkles?

One woman might see her wrinkles purely as signs of age and sadness. Another woman the same exact age might interpret those lines as sparkles of experience and wisdom.

What's the difference between these women? The first sees the past and years of living as hardships. The second views the same number of years as signs of accomplishment and lessons learned to share with others. Which of these two women is happier and will go on to accomplish even greater things?

The obvious answer is number two. Here's the shocker: for years, I related more to number one because I was in that boat right along with her. For many years, despite having had a successful career as an international model and actress, I was the woman who secretly viewed her life as a half-empty, cracked glass.

It's well documented that many people in the public eye can't seem to handle the stress of fame and recognition. All you have to do is look at the tabloids to find out about the latest star who has been arrested or checked into rehab. Models, actresses, and anyone else who has slinked down the runway, graced the Broadway stage, or glittered across the big screen may seem superconfident and glamorous on the outside but are often frail, anxious, and nervous people on the inside. I've had a bird's-eye view of many modeling and acting sensations soaring to astronomical heights and then tumbling down because they didn't have a strong inner foundation of self-esteem.

I am not in any way glamorizing celebrity or its pitfalls. I don't pretend that models and entertainers are any better than anyone else, suffer more, or require extra sympathy. In fact, we are all just like you, in spite of how confidently we present and flaunt ourselves.

Speaking for myself, this is what I *can* say: like you, I have had more than my share of hard knocks and insecurities going back to my childhood. I *can't* say whether my self-esteem issues were innate, ingrained in me by others, a result of circumstances, or a combination of all these factors.

I was a relatively quiet and reserved girl, but I had big dreams. When I was granted permission and the house was peaceful, I watched classic old films featuring starlets like Ava Gardner and Rita Hayworth. How I loved them! I wanted to *be* them. When I was chosen for the role of Mary Poppins in the kindergarten play, I became certain that one day I would have a shot at starring in movies, too.

Alas, the looks that brought me my first "star turn" didn't last long. I regressed from a cute five-year-old into a lanky, flat-chested adolescent with buckteeth and protruding ears. (Don't believe me? I have the pictures to prove it!)

Mirror, Mirror

My life went straight downhill from there. I never thought I would be pretty. I didn't even think anyone would ever want to look at me. My dreams of being in movies faded with every passing year.

Little by little, my looks improved. In my case the cliché was true: I blossomed from an ugly duckling into a swan and started to get noticed.

Before I knew it, I was being hired for modeling assignments. I moved to Italy in the 1980s and became one of the top runway models in the world, alongside such icons as Iman and Jerry Hall. I appeared on more than one hundred magazine covers and even had my own cosmetics counter at Bloomingdale's for a decade. I was high in demand for ad campaigns with Revlon, Helen Rubenstein, Dior, and many others. My acting career soon followed. I was making money and living a glamorous lifestyle I'd never dreamed possible. What could possibly go wrong?

Tripping on the Runway of Life

Everything went wrong. The problem? I didn't believe that I deserved any of my success. Somewhere buried deep down I still felt like that ugly duckling and that someone was going to "out" me as a fraud.

On top of that, I was ill equipped to find my way on my own in the real world, and I was an easy target. Relationships with men were difficult and painful. Sure, these guys wanted a pretty model on their arms—but they didn't care to know a thing about me and certainly didn't love me. Come to think of it—did I even feel like I *deserved* to be loved?

I placed all of the blame on myself and faced my first major depression at twenty-six years of age. I searched everywhere for answers, reading every self-help book I could find. Then I had a revelation.

The REgime to the Rescue

One day, when I was in the midst of producing the Miss Universe Pageant, I looked around and noticed something: many of these beautiful women standing around me were suffering from the same self-esteem issues that I was.

I started speaking with girls and women outside the modeling and entertainment industries—all sizes, shapes, looks, ethnicities, professions, and social and economic statuses—around the world and discovered that they, too, were struggling to feel confident and good about themselves.

Aha! I realized. *Low self-esteem is universal!*

Like many women, I had been placing all of my self-worth on my physical appearance and how I thought others viewed me. But how does a person reverse negative self-perception that is so ingrained in the psyche? It would take a hard-edged approach to counter all of the noise in my head and years of baggage. It was like I needed a military sergeant in my head to shout at me and drill out all of the swirling negative thoughts. Through trial and error, I developed a comprehensive program for myself that provided answers and solutions. At long last, I could look myself in the mirror without worrying that a monkey was going to jump out at me. I felt good about my reflection and the person I had become.

Unfortunately, as I became more self-assured, confident, and strong, I continued to feel empty. I knew something was still missing: what about all of the women I had encountered over the years who were grappling with low self-esteem? I felt compelled to reach out, share my discoveries, and embark on an all-out mission to help others.

The Self-Esteem REgime was born.

You Deserve to Look Good and Feel Good Right Now: The Four Pillars

Although I had created my regime by accident, you have the opportunity to complete it with intent and purpose. My goal is to help you to break through your personal obstacles, defeat your inner demons, and feel good about yourself. You *deserve* to achieve everything your heart desires and more.

Before you experience your personal rebirth, I would like to introduce to you what I refer to as "The Four Pillars for Living an Esteemed Life." I suggest you turn this invaluable credo into a screensaver on your phone or print it out and tape it to your laptop or computer screen. I can't emphasize how valuable these Four Pillars will be to begin your reinvention: *Look Good, Feel Good, Be Good, Greater Good*. Repeat these to yourself several times a day—especially when you are feeling less than whole.

Look Good

When you truly believe you look good, you know it. This feeling shows through and does wonders for your self-esteem. With this mind-set, you can strut in public like you are a runway model. Color, proportion, and personal style all play a big part in your overall look. When I was a beauty editor, I scoured beauty trade shows for the latest and the greatest information to nurture *inner beauty*, which extends to outward beauty.

Feel Good

You can't look good if you don't feel good, right? Proper diet and exercise are critical in helping you to feel fantastic and more energetic. If you treat your body right, you will look good, and your mind will respond right back with positive thoughts.

Be Good

We all want to be our best in our business and personal lives. Continuing education and learning are paramount to living an esteemed life. This doesn't mean browsing TikTok, Facebook, Instagram, Pinterest, Twitter, or any other social media flavor of the day. I'm not suggesting you can't be active in social media in small doses, but often the posts of others offer misinformation or waste your precious time and rot your brain cells on trivial matters. Worse, some posts, apps, and quizzes have the opposite impact on self-esteem, causing you to feel like you aren't measuring up to others or living the exciting lives of the people in your social network. Being good is what you do to enrich your mind and soul. You can be good to yourself by doing simple activities such as yoga, going for walks, meditating, reading books, joining a reading group, and many other fun things we'll discuss.

Greater Good

Last, but certainly not least: there is no greater boost for your self-esteem than doing something good for someone else. It's remarkable how good a person feels when helping others out by volunteering, tithing (donating one tenth of your earnings), and teaching others. There are so many wonderful ways to give back, which we'll cover in the final chapter of the regime.

How Tough Is *The Self-Esteem REgime*?

The Self-Esteem REgime will make you mentally and emotionally tough, but you have no worries in terms of the demands it will make on you. The intention is for the regime to be enlightening and empowering but by no means is it grueling in the military sense.

The prefix *re-* is a vital component of this book. By definition, "*re-*" originates from ancient Latin and connotes occurring "again" or "again and again" to indicate repetition. Since for many people the human brain is wired at birth and molded during the development years to think a certain way, we cling to perspectives that may not be true but end up being sustained as fact because our thinking has become rigid. By aggressively targeting poor self-perception and blasting negative thoughts with reverse concepts over and over, the mind gets a reboot and the universe opens up through a new light. This barrage of mental assertions, which ultimately become new, sustainable thought, is the revolutionary essence of my regime.

Through a dozen progressive building steps comprising the regime and emphasizing the "re-" concept, you will discover newfound power, energy, confidence, and happiness:

RElease. REbuild. REsponsibility. REplace. REaffirm. REinvent.
REinforce. REpeat. REbound. REdirect. REspect. REciprocal.

By the end of the book, you will become so recharged and revitalized that you will be able to build a powerful regime of your own to reign over: how you regard your self-image; how you are viewed by others; and how you can convert your newfound respect into success. My mission is to help you optimize the way you look, how you feel about yourself, and how you handle yourself in all interactions.

You deserve to become happier, healthier, and more prosperous. You deserve to be in total control of your destiny. By incorporating these concepts into your life, you will become the person everyone looks at in awe each and every time you enter the room.

CHAPTER ONE

~

RElease

The time has come to lay that baggage down and leave behind all the struggling and striving.

—Sue Augustine, author

Margot is a bright, friendly, and attractive college graduate. Despite her gifts, her lack of social skills and sensitive nature have made it difficult for her to sustain friendships over the years. Throughout junior high, high school, and college, Margot inadvertently said and texted things that upset her friends. As a result, they stopped responding to her and literally unfriended her.

Margot lands her first full-time job in a completely different state where she doesn't know anyone and feels she can have a fresh start. At work, people treat her respectfully, but no one seems interested in a friendship with her. Margot is too shy and bookish to initiate conversations that are unrelated to job functions.

In the evening, she finds herself alone and afraid. She thinks about all of the times over the years her so-called friends never returned her calls and texts. She pictures her most embarrassing moments with girls from junior high and high school and berates herself: "Stupid, stupid, stupid! Why did I say those things?"

Will Margot ever release herself from the past?

We live in a tough world. No doubt you have felt some anger, frustration, disillusionment, or disappointment in your life. It's compounded by our social and political climate, in which racial diatribes and name-calling have become the norm.

What are your beliefs about life and yourself in this moment? Are they working for you? Have you fulfilled all of your dreams? Do you have the career you want? Are you unhappy with how you look, perhaps your weight? Could you be making healthier choices? Are the relationships in your life—romantic partners, siblings, parents, children, extended family, friends, coworkers, and so on—making you happy and healthy or bringing you down?

If not, it's obvious that the old way of doing things isn't working for you anymore. You may be stuck like Margot, the young woman introduced at the beginning of this chapter. Her story is truly heartbreaking. Although there is nothing wrong with being an introvert and focusing on "me time," it's also not healthy to feel alone, helpless, and buried in the past, the same patterns repeating over and over.

As we are now in the first stage of the regime, it's time for Margot—and you—to release some baggage. Most of the things from our past that continue to bother us and fester serve no purpose other than to hold us back. They are detrimental to moving forward and often result in low self-esteem. It's time for you to get rid of old habits and confining feelings and start anew.

It may be comforting for you to know that very few people's lives are perfectly in order. Take heart in the fact that you are not alone. Many of the people you see as "having their acts together" are probably just pretending.

I'm not going to sugarcoat things and say everything is perfectly fine and hunky-dory in your life and the world at large. There's a lot of garbage out there! Reminders of the past continue to pop up and haunt us. New stressors constantly surface. But you must learn to *control the controllables*—that is, the things within your world that you can change and influence while ignoring the rest—and release negative thought patterns that restrict you and hold you back. You need to wipe that slate clean and start anew, pretending today is the start of a new year. Take a leap of faith that all will be okay.

Let's get started!

We Are All Imperfect

Do you remember the popular girls in junior high and high school? They were cheerleaders, had hunky boyfriends on the football team, wore trendy clothes, and seemed to always know the right things to say. They seemed happy, at least on the surface. Do you believe their fantasy school facades extended to their private lives? Do you think they didn't have insecurities of their own and embarrassing secrets that they kept hidden? Do you think they kept their looks over the years, went on to earn fame and fortune, and lived happily ever after in the burbs with their high school jock sweethearts?

Chances are, this scenario is far from the case. *Everyone* faces challenges, heartaches, and stumbling blocks at one time or another. The girls you thought "had it all" back in junior high and high school experienced their own set of issues and neuroses. How do I know this as fact? Because *everyone* does.

I don't offer this to become high and mighty about the downfalls and struggles of people from your past—even those whom you think deserve it because they mistreated you in some way. It may feel good to be smug for a while, but that is not the path to strong self-esteem. If anything, you should forgive them for what they did to you, whether their harmful behaviors were intentional or not. You don't know the full story of what they went through in the past, and it's entirely possible that they have changed their ways and matured over the years. Perhaps they even regret some of their remarks and detrimental behavior toward you (or having ignored or dropped you entirely).

Most importantly, by acknowledging that the people you viewed as sitting atop Mount Olympus were (and are) imperfect mere mortals, you release the demons that have haunted you over the years. *No one* is perfect, *no one* has led the perfect life, *no one* has made perfect decisions, and *no one* is without sin. You shouldn't expend an ounce of energy comparing yourself to anyone—past or present—especially if it means belittling yourself.

Margot—the young woman cited earlier—may have made some unintentional mistakes in the past. So what? The so-called friends who had ghosted her were shallow and therefore not worth their salt. They didn't "get" Margot and it's their loss. True friends not only look after each other, they also can see past their faults and love and support each other anyway.

If you are in any way like Margot, it is time to find the kindness in your heart to forgive and release. You must let go of those who caused you pain and stop being afraid the new people you encounter will treat you the same way. Why assume they would cause you harm? They don't know a thing about you! You always have a chance to start over with a clean slate as long as you have purged your own baggage.

We all have the light in us, and no one in the world has the right to extinguish it. Give yourself the gift of forgiveness. Whatever you said or did in the past to lose friendships was probably not nearly as bad as you think.

As for Margot, it is time for her to live and enjoy life to the fullest. I don't expect her to become an extrovert overnight or even believe she needs hordes of friends to feel good about herself and fill her void. A couple of true, reliable friends who appreciate her for the person she is would be more than enough.

Yet Margot must recognize that the break room at work is not the school cafeteria and that no one will embarrass or drop her like her former so-called friends. She can sit at a table and have a casual cup of coffee with a colleague—or even ask her if she wants to go out for a quick drink after work when it's mutually convenient. I don't know any respectable adult who would ever say "no" to such a harmless, friendly invite—especially from a sweet, one-of a-kind person like Margot!

Sensitive People Are Strong People

Some of Margot's social issues are fairly common among highly sensitive people (HSP), a term coined by Elaine N. Aron, PhD. It's estimated that 15 to 20 percent of people are highly sensitive to varying degrees, whether diagnosed or not. As it happens, HPS is something I share in common with Margot. I found it to be a great comfort when I discovered that some of the unusual things that I had been experiencing were medically explainable. I cannot tolerate bright lights or any kind of loud noises—from pounding music to barking dogs to crying babies. I have difficulty with scents, too. I can't be in a restaurant where there are pungent smells or smoke in the air. (For this reason,

I won't cook in my own home.) I'm also extremely sensitive to touch, especially on my scalp. This extends to emotional reactions as well; my senses won't tolerate any kind of scary movie, and I admit to not having seen one since 1979.

You can imagine how all of this made my life difficult as a model and actress. Bright camera lights always caused some measure of trauma. Loud music at events and shows caused great discomfort. Hairdressers were always way too rough with my hair.

I'm not making excuses for myself but—when I was exposed to such environmental conditions—I admit that I acted in a manner some might refer to as "bitchy" and became difficult to work with. By simply recognizing that I am an HPS, I have learned how to avoid certain situations or temper my behavior when my senses betray me.

Margot, who tends to react to overwhelming situations by withdrawing and looking pained, has learned to identify her behaviors the moment they flare up. She heads to the nearest private, quiet place—a restroom or outdoors, if possible—closes her eyes, and takes ten relaxing breaths before reentering the fray. She also gently explains to people in advance that loud sounds, lights, and crowds are difficult for her so that people won't be surprised if she exhibits unusual behaviors.

I'm not suggesting that you are an HSP, but if you have any of the aforementioned symptoms, it may be worth checking with your medical practitioner. Many people with HSP do happen to also have self-esteem issues. The good news is that your quality of life need not suffer another minute longer!

The Power to Let Go Is within Your Grasp

We have all become so reliant on our phones and laptops that we often forget the most cathartic activity of all: writing things down.

There is nothing quite like taking pen to paper. The physical act of jotting things down releases your inner thoughts and emotions in a way that tapping on a phone cannot. I suggest taking some extra time to select just the right pen that feels good in your hand, writes smoothly, and allows thoughts to bubble up naturally. Similarly, browse your favorite stationery or gift store and pick up a notebook that has just the right look and feel in your hand. It could be small or large; ruled or unruled; or spiral bound, leather bound, or with plain cardboard binding. The journal could contain words from your favorite inspirational authors or historical figures or perhaps illustrated with fancy drawings and graphics. Or maybe it features a fancy ribbon and has a magnetized cover. The choice is yours: make it feel as personal to you as possible.

Once you have the perfect pen and journal, place it on top of or inside your night table. When you wake up every morning (after a bathroom break, of course), write freely in it for ten minutes. The substance of what you write doesn't matter. It could be a dream, thoughts that kept you staring at the ceiling all night, or random creative ideas. Even if you are a stickler for grammar, do not edit yourself or revise the language at all. Let the words flow and any spelling and punctuation errors pass.

I know what you are thinking: *I need those extra ten minutes of sleep!* In response to that, I say: *What have those extra ten minutes of sleep achieved for you in terms of being able to release your emotional baggage?* Not much, right?

At the end of the day, before going to sleep, grab that journal and continue writing for another ten minutes. Don't even think of raising the "I'm too tired" objection. What else are you going to do with those ten minutes? Stare at Facebook posts and Instagram photos on your phone? (We'll discuss the value of waking up an hour earlier later in the regime.)

At the end of each week—not before—grab a highlighter (any color) and drag the tip through the things that continue to dog you from the past. They could be setbacks, failures, embarrassing moments, mistakes, shortcomings, criticisms you've received—anything negative that has remained stuck in your mind. If a painful event, thought, or feeling from the past recurs more than once, put an asterisk next to each instance.

Take a fresh sheet of paper and transcribe onto it everything you've highlighted. Also be sure to copy the asterisks. In a private, comforting space, do the following:

1. Read each memory, thought, or emotion aloud, one at a time.
2. Before moving on to the next one, close your eyes.
3. Visualize what you have written.

4. Open your eyes.
5. Strike a line through it.
6. Move on to the next one and repeat steps 1 through 5.
7. After you have completed steps 1 through 6, crumple up and toss out the paper (not your journal, of course).

By coming to terms with and then obliterating your past in this manner, you are effectively adding much-needed closure to the thoughts and memories that continue to hurt you. You deserve to find peace, rid yourself of these terrible things, and, finally, be able to move forward. If it's a case of exorcising someone who hurt you long ago, why would you want that person to continue to have a hold over you after so much time has elapsed?

Dominating Your Daily Demons

If the past continues to flare up in your writings, you can try an alternative approach. Once again, highlight the things in your journal that have been on your mind that week. Copy them onto a sheet of paper, but this time leave space after each one. When you've finished, go back to the top and write down something positive that has come out of that negative. It could be a mistake you learned never to repeat, a new career path, or a happier relationship. By replacing negative with positive, you are disposing of your demon forever.

Say NO to No

Without exception, being told "No" is a painful experience for everyone. As a model and actress, I can tell you firsthand what it feels like to be passed over for opportunities you really want. These turndowns can ring in your head like an old tape, looping over and over again, especially if they involve being on the receiving end of harsh criticism.

Be aware, however, that the people who turn you down may not be the right fit for what you are trying to achieve—whether you are an actor, writer, painter, entrepreneur, or anything else. They simply might not "get you." Or, perhaps, the people with decision-making power are flat-out wrong. People make mistakes. They miss things. You may be ahead of your time. These people who rejected your work (not you, of course) are only human, after all. Believe me, people miscast actors all of the time in the entertainment industry. Just look at all of the box-office turkeys that get released each year and don't even make it to cable!

History is filled with examples of geniuses who were turned down. Vincent Van Gogh painted more than two thousand works but only sold about a couple in his lifetime and lived in squalor. The Beatles were spurned by several major recording companies before they were signed by producer George Martin at EMI. Stephen King's classic novel *Carrie* was turned down no less than thirty times before an acquisitions editor at Doubleday finally "got it." Back in 1976, Dino De Laurentiis described a young actress as an "ugly thing" and rejected her for the starring role in *King Kong*. The name of that actress? Meryl Streep— before she became a multi-Oscar winner!

I believe that rejection is *essential* in order to find your way to success. The people who most seem like "overnight successes" are the ones who received thousands of rejections, paid their dues through blood, sweat, and tears, and yet persevered anyway. If you give up on your dream after one or two negative reactions, it means you aren't meant to achieve it because you didn't have enough skin in the game.

Clar-ion Call

Think of a "no" as a building block to creating the foundations of your dream. Every time you receive a rejection, imagine that you are one block closer to making it a reality. Success is a numbers game! The more blocks you build, the greater likelihood you will strike it big.

We are all human beings, and I understand that facing constant rejection can seem frustrating and hopeless. I've been there, done that, and have come to realize that stewing about it won't get you anywhere. Every time you receive a "no," shout "NO!" right back at it and keep right on going.

Never give up. Never stop believing in your goals and dreams. You don't owe the "no's" a darn thing. The people who turned you down forgot about you the moment you stepped out the door; they didn't give you a second thought. Why should you continue to let the rejection rattle in your head when that person couldn't care less?

Clarissa's Corner

Let's rephrase the expression "The 'no's' have it" to "The 'no's' have *had* it!"
Buh-bye, "no's"!

Don't Allow Judgmental Family Members a Place in Your Head

Parents love their children and always want the best for them. Siblings care deeply for each other and cheer them on. Why is it, then, that family members always seem to cause the pain that lingers the longest and is hardest to release?

Parents are so emotionally attuned and connected to their children that they often lack objectivity about how they interact with them. Yes, there could be a personality issue involved on their part or they simply may be jealous of your success, but, for now, let's give them the benefit of the doubt. In good faith—no matter how awkward, twisted, or hurtful—they may be thinking that they are offering well-meaning advice to you when, in fact, they are inadvertently taking you down several notches.

Mothers, fathers, sisters, brothers, grandparents, cousins, and even close friends are human beings. Some are able to self-reflect, but most cannot—especially when it comes to loved ones. They simply cannot be objective with you because they expect you to be perfect and may not like how you resemble *them*. Or perhaps they don't want you to commit the same mistakes they did.

Do not let anyone burst your bubble! Let's suppose your dream has always been to be a professional writer. You know the hurdles it will take to become successful—both in terms of the craft and monetizing it—but you have the passion and believe you also possess the skill. Now comes the hard work. You've spent years writing and honing your talent. You complete the manuscript for your book and then share it with your mother. After having read it she says, "It's *so good*, dear. But do you think someone really will be interested in publishing something like this? You've spent so many years on it, don't you think it's time for you to get a job that pays?"

Your mother has praised your work (sort of), but what words do you remember? Three things: no one will be interested in publishing it; you'll never make money; and you wasted your time on it. Your mother thinks she is providing helpful guidance and feedback, but she is actually popping your bubblegum bubble, and it's splattering all over your face.

No matter what your dream might be or how much you value the opinions of family and friends, do not ever allow them to yank you down from your cloud. Here is the truth: in the above circumstance of the critical mother, ask yourself, *Is she an expert on great writing? Is she a literary agent? Is she an editor at a publishing house?* Presuming the answer is "no," there isn't any reason whatsoever to take her comments to heart. She has no idea whether your book is commercial enough to sell to a publisher or whether people would buy it once it's out.

Often the comments stem from things said during childhood. We may be grown-up adults in our forties, fifties, sixties, or beyond, but a snide comment made by a parent when we were ten years old reverberates in our heads as if it was said an hour ago. Things stated by our parents during our formative years can feel much more severe than those by a total stranger—even if they don't hold any water.

If you have a family member or friend who brought you down in the past and/or continues to do so, try to avoid sharing details of your goal and journey with that person until you have met with success. If it comes up in conversation (i.e., "How is your book coming along?"), do not engage in the dialogue except to smile and say, "Very well, thank you. I appreciate your asking." That's it. Limiting this exchange helps protect you from potentially hearing words that diminish your enthusiasm.

On the other hand, if you have family members and friends who form a genuine support team for you, focus on those relationships instead. By all means, lean on them when you need a boost. The best thing you can do for yourself is to develop a posse of cheerleaders who understand you and provide unrequited loyalty and encouragement.

It's inevitable, though, that negative voices and baggage will re-emerge when you least expect them and control your thoughts when you are at your weakest. As a means of daily release—for both prevention and reversal during flare-ups—I suggest you recite the affirmation below aloud at least twice a day (preferably morning and evening).

In advance of Thanksgiving, Christmas, or other family get-togethers where you know critical family members will be ready to pounce on you, recite the affirmation three times to yourself beforehand in the mirror. When the zingers come your way, say it in your head with the intent of drowning out what you are hearing. Smile and nod at your attacker while pretending to listen.

Whatever you do, you must not be lured into an argument or attempt to defend yourself. There is no way to win this battle, and it's not worth it. Why? Because you already know you are a champion!

Affirmation: My Life Depends upon It

I honor myself . . . my life depends upon it.
My voice is all that matters . . . my life depends upon it.
Negative voices of past and present are like a wind that comes, goes, and never returns . . . my life depends upon it.
I am my biggest fan . . . my life depends upon it.
I deserve success . . . my life depends upon it.
I honor the good and caring people who cheer me on, no matter what . . . my life depends upon it.

REview

- Release the baggage that holds you back in order to move forward and find success.
- Keep a journal by your bedside to write down—and later smack down—the thoughts, feelings, and words that bother you.
- Recognize that being told "no" is merely one building block toward creating your towering wall of success.

- Refuse to allow negative comments from family, friends, or anyone else to dictate your mind-set.
- Recite the "My Life Depends upon It" affirmation to purge negative voices and to prevent new ones from registering.

CHAPTER TWO

~

REbuild

Leap and the net will appear.

—John Burroughs, American nature essayist

Several years ago, I befriended a twenty-two-year-old Las Vegas call girl named Tiffany who was in dire straits and desperate to escape from her dangerous environment. I welcomed her into my home in Arizona for four months, where she physically separated from her former life with the intent of figuring out how to start anew. While she was in this protective cocoon, we worked together on her reinvention. She had already begun to release a hefty amount of baggage—mainly shame and guilt over what she had become and some resentment toward her mother. They had a poor relationship, which she believes led to her ending up in Vegas.

"I don't want to be thought of as a call girl anymore," she cried to me. "I never want anyone to look, think, or talk about me in that way ever again. I'm sick of the labels."

"Other people can't tell you who you are," I consoled her. "Only you can do that for yourself. Let's figure it out—together."

Desperate to eradicate her call girl label, we went item by item through the things that connected to her prior lifestyle. She ditched her phone, replaced it, and got an unlisted number and different area code, so no one from her past could ever track her down.

I noticed that her car was flashy and sent out the wrong impression to the world. We removed her glittery "bling" license plate holder and painted over the punkish racing stripe on the side of the vehicle. For good measure, we had the interior of the vehicle thoroughly detailed.

Next, we worked on her physical appearance. She was naturally gorgeous and voluptuous, but that didn't mean she had to wear cleavage-revealing tops, tight leather pants, or ridiculously high heels. She swapped those things out with smart, attractive everyday women's clothes from the Gap and Anne Taylor Loft.

Last, we stripped her down, as it were, removing unnecessary layers of makeup, long eyelashes, and wig. The transformation was nothing short of breathtaking—like Julia Roberts in the film Pretty Woman.

"I love it," Tiffany said, glancing at her new identity in a full-length mirror. "I look like a totally different person . . . but . . . the problem is, now I don't know who I am."

"You've made excellent progress," I complimented her. "You're officially ready for the next stage in your makeover—rebuilding."

Your situation may not be as extreme as Tiffany's, and I'm certainly not making any assumptions or judgments regarding your career or lifestyle. Her story does, however, bear relevance as you continue your self-esteem journey. Like Tiffany, you have reached the second stage of the regime and need to claim—or, more precisely, reclaim—your identity. Even if you think you know who you are, chances are that you don't because the "real you" has been submerged. If you have been suffering from low self-esteem, you have probably been living according to the labels foisted on to you by other people. Some of these may be less-than-flattering monikers regarding your intelligence and/ or appearance. Others may reflect only a piece—though perhaps an important one—of the total person you really are: mother, wife, sister, spouse, and so forth. Then there is the label attached to your current job—that is, waitress, supermarket cashier, housekeeper, office assistant, and so on—which helps make ends meet but does not define you. Even though you've continued to serve in this role for many years, you feel the job is not your "career."

Are you living according to the expectations or preconceived notions of others? It doesn't have to be this way. You can rebuild yourself! Like most things worth attaining, it takes time, patience, and work. But isn't striving to become the person you've always wanted to be worth the effort?

We Can Become the People We Were Meant to Be

I don't care if you are in your teens, twenties, fifties, sixties, seventies, or beyond. There is always time to find your true identity—or, more precisely, to unleash it from within.

Starting out fresh may be scary—particularly when you are trying to pinpoint your identity—but it can also be a liberating and exhilarating experience. Just imagine that you are the director, producer, and actor of your own film and control how you view yourself in the camera lens and what ends up projected on the screen.

In the beginning, every movie requires a vision, and your life is no different. Whether you wish for the story of your life to be accomplished, financially rewarding, or just plain enjoyable is entirely up to you. Whatever you truly desire must be completely planned out in your mind's eye and memorialized in such a way that it becomes all-consuming for you at all times—even while you are asleep. Appropriately, it all starts with a dream.

Rekindle Your Dream

When you were a child, what did you dream about? Did you want to become an astronaut? An internationally acclaimed dancer? A star soccer player? A painter? Or just wealthy?

The dream didn't necessarily have to revolve around fame, fortune, or creative accomplishment. You might have longed to become a professional such a nurse, doctor, teacher, architect, chef, or business owner but your ambitions were thrown off course. All of these are wonderful aspirations and there is no right or wrong. The question remains: are you living your original dream in some direct or indirect way or has it faded into the recesses of your mind and been overtaken by other priorities?

Whether you realize it or not, your dream still lurks inside you and is desperate to be released. If it doesn't come to fruition in some fashion, you will feel a void deep inside and won't have a chance to feel good about yourself. A sense of disappointment will continue to linger and fester.

This brings us back to Tiffany's story and her rebuilding process. While shedding her previous persona, we worked on establishing beneficial routines that would form a solid new foundation for her. I became something of a nonjudgmental "cool aunt" to her, providing her with positive affirmations and making sure that she had what she needed, was living cleanly, practiced good sleeping habits, and took responsibility for her living quarters (making her bed) and other areas, such as the bathroom (keeping it clean) and kitchen (not leaving dishes and utensils in the sink). Not only did she wake up at a reasonable hour in a comfortable setting, we adjusted her diet so she would eat berries and other wholesome foods every morning and throughout the day.

Clar-ion Call

Right from the start of your regime, keep your possessions organized. I know, I probably sound like your mother. The truth of the matter is that good organization is one of the keys to feeling as though you have your life under control. Most tasks, such as wiping the sink after brushing your teeth, are easy enough to do and surefire ways to jump-start your morning.

After a few days of separating herself from her past and adjusting, Tiffany sat down on my living room couch while I stood in front of a dry erase board with a marker at the ready. "When you were little, what did you want to be? What did you dream about?"

She thought this over for a while until her face curved into a semi-embarrassed smile.

"What is it?" I demanded. "Come on, you can share it with me."

"You'll laugh," she blushed.

"I promise, I won't."

"Okay," she said, sitting more upright. "I've always loved doing makeup and hair. Not just for myself, but my friends, too. I really loved doing it. I think my friends thought I was good at it. We all pretended we worked at a salon."

"Perfect!" I exclaimed, writing several words on the board:

TIFFANY'S DREAM
Makeup. Hair. Salon.

She lit up seeing her name on the board associated with those words. "I love those things, but they weren't really what I fantasized about becoming."

"Okay," I said, lowering the marker. "What did you fantasize about becoming?"

She blushed, laughing hysterically at herself.

"I don't understand. Why is your fantasy so funny?" I asked.

She continued to attempt to contain herself. "Um . . . I mean . . . Clarissa, you've modeled professionally on runways all around the world. I'm sure you think it's a ridiculous idea for me, given who I am—I mean, *was*."

"You dreamed about being a model? It's not funny or ridiculous at all! Remember, we already unloaded your baggage. It's *gone*," I insisted.

"I know. But being a model like you? You're so beautiful and glamorous," she countered. "I'm nowhere near that level."

"Don't *ever* say that about yourself," I cautioned her. "You are blessed with sensational looks. I would go as far as saying you are positively *stunning*. In fact, you are ten times prettier than I ever was."

She sat up straight, soaking in what I was saying. I scribbled the word *model* prominently across the center of the board. "It's never too late to work toward fulfilling your dream. You just need to build your confidence and get some basic things done to get started, such as creating a portfolio. It happens that I know a photographer who owes me a favor. I also have connections at a local modeling agency. I'm sure they'd be happy to consider you."

"Really?" she clapped her hands with excitement. "You would do that for me?"

"Absolutely!"

Tiffany and I made an appointment with Darren, my photographer friend. He was happy to oblige us by spending a full day taking a range of photos of her, including both headshots and fashion shots of her modeling swimwear, dresses, and other items—but nothing too risqué. The photographs turned out exceptionally well. Tiffany couldn't have been more pleased with herself and how she looked.

Next, I set her up with the local modeling agency, where she had an opportunity to present her portfolio. She was a trooper throughout the long waits between meetings in reception; the deliberations among the executives; the interviewing process; and so forth. A fetching young assistant ushered us out with hugs and said, "Thank you so much. We have everything we need. We'll call you if anything comes up."

I could see Tiffany's heart sink as we went down in the elevator. "They aren't really going to call me, are they," she murmured.

"You never know," I assured her, not wishing to burst her bubble. "Listen, it took a lot of strength and courage to do what you did. And you were *awesome*. Whatever happens, you should count this as a major accomplishment."

"Okay," she said unconvincingly as tears formed in her eyes.

When we returned to my home, we headed straight for the living room and picked up where we left off. I stood at the board with a marker as she situated herself on the couch. "Let me ask you this question, Tiffany. Be honest with yourself. Did you enjoy the modeling process?"

"Some of it, I guess," she replied. "I didn't like all of the waiting around for the photographer to set up the shots . . . or all of the fussing to get my positioning and expressions right . . . a lot of it was kind of boring. And I didn't really care much for the people at the modeling agency—they all seemed so . . . *phony*."

"Welcome to the world of modeling!" I laughed. "Tell me, what *did* you like?"

"I really liked all of the preparation stuff," she answered. "Putting my makeup on . . . doing my hair . . . all of that."

I circled the words *makeup* and *hair*, which had already been scribbled on the board. "You know, Tiffany, everything you say seems to come back to these two things. You light up when we talk about them."

She perked up. "You're right!"

"With that in mind, what is it you *really* want to do?"

She hesitated at first, but then the words came charging out: "*I want to help women look as beautiful as they can be.*"

"That's it—you've done it!" I exclaimed, writing her exact words across the board.

"Done what?"

"You have identified your *purpose.*"

She stared at her newfound purpose with fascination, allowing the words to fully sink in. "I can't believe it . . . those words say it exactly. I've felt it inside my whole life but didn't realize it. So . . . what do we do now?"

"Your first rebuilding block is in place—your purpose," I stated. "It's exciting—but it means your work has only just begun. Are you ready to continue your journey?"

"Hell, yeah!"

Identifying Your Purpose

Your purpose statement is a sentence or two that defines your *why*— that is, the fuel that drives your passion. In Tiffany's case, it wasn't just about "doing makeup and hair," it was about the motivation behind those physical tasks. She wanted to *help others* to look and feel good. A purpose becomes even more potent when it goes from the inside—not just focusing on oneself—and shines outward to the world.

As it turned out, Tiffany did receive a couple of modest modeling assignments. She performed well on both occasions but, as I suspected, didn't get any satisfaction from them whatsoever. The work itself was unfulfilling for her; quite simply, her heart wasn't in it.

She continued to study and understand her purpose, writing it down in her journal and visualizing what that might look like if it were to be realized.

Clarissa's Corner

Write your purpose down everywhere you can: in your journal; as a screensaver on your laptop or desktop; on a Post-It on your desk; as a beautiful printout on your refrigerator; and everywhere else. This defines who you are—be proud of it!

Tiffany experienced a raw moment of self-awareness. On deeper reflection, she realized that becoming a model may have seemed like a nice fantasy, but it wasn't her true underlying dream. Once she arrived at this conclusion, she was able to home in on her passion and make that her sole focus. With all of this positive emotion and power embedded in her purpose, we knew that nothing was ever going to stand in her way. The right purpose is so strong that it can ensure you stay the course, no matter what setbacks and obstacles might come your way.

Your *why* is, in fact, your *superpower*.

Mission *Possible*

Now that Tiffany had memorialized her purpose, it was time to add on the next block of her rebuilding project: her *mission*.

"It sounds like something religious," she joked.

"Well, I guess it could be," I said. "But really it's about thinking of yourself in terms of a business."

"A business? What do you mean?" she asked.

"Every business operates in a certain way in order to make money and profit. There are certain things a company must do each and every day from the start in order to get off the ground and sustain itself. In your case, you want to elaborate on your purpose—*I want to help women look as beautiful as they can be*—in such a way that every action you take accomplishes it. Your mission is what you set out to do every day to fulfill your purpose."

Once she had grasped the concept, we brainstormed and wordsmithed language for several hours until we came up with the perfect simplified verbiage:

Mission
To use my makeup and hairstyling skills in order to help women look and feel their best

Bingo! Mission accomplished.

Becoming the Visionary of Your Life

It isn't enough just to have a purpose and mission. You know *what* you are going to do and *why* you are doing it—but do you know *where* you are going? If you don't, you could pursue the wrong path and get lost or perhaps even crash into a brick wall.

This is why we all need a vision: it guides us where we are headed at all times. You can think of it in terms of a compass or GPS that reminds you of your direction, so you always make it safely to your destination.

For your personal vision, you must imagine where you long to be at least five years from now (it could be more). This is your final destination on your journey, which means it needs to represent your ultimate success story and lead to happiness and fulfillment.

For Tiffany, correctly identifying this was an essential part of her rebuilding process. Once she locked and loaded her purpose and mission, she knew exactly where she wanted to go to end up at the finish line.

Vision
To become a professional makeup artist and hairstylist and own my own salon.

"Wow," I marveled. "That is an ambitious vision."

"Oh no!" she reacted. "Have I gone too far?"

"Au contraire!" I shouted. "It's the *ideal* vision for you. A vision *should* be ambitious. Don't get me wrong, though, it's going to take a lot of unbelievably hard work. But the good thing is that if you keep focusing on your purpose, mission, and vision, you will never go off course."

The Vision Is Your Movie
Near the beginning of this chapter, I described how visualizing your future life can help you become the person you are meant to be. This is where you take hold of the camera and start projecting!

Every film starts off with a premise and a concept. (In film lingo, this becomes known as the *logline* or *pitch*.) Your stated vision already serves this function, guiding you to metaphorically write the script for your film. In this case, think more in terms of an animated storyboard than an actual written screenplay.

Technically, your storyboard is—*drumroll, please*—your vision board. It looks and feels exactly like the movie of your future life captured in one visual snapshot. You can utilize whatever "canvas" you see fit: a corkboard, a dry erase board (recognizing that this isn't permanent), oak tag, or literal painting canvas. You can even create an old-school diorama, if you are so inclined.

The idea is to create it in such a manner that it looks like what you see in your mind's eye. The items you incorporate on (or in) it can be an avant-garde assemblage of random photographs, cutouts, drawings, or words. There are only three pieces of instruction: the items must all fit into your purpose, mission, and vision; the final version needs to be placed near you (i.e., where you work) as much as possible; and the end result should look like the happy final scene of your film, a.k.a. your ideal personal journey.

You probably are asking the questions: *Does Clarissa Burt have a vision board? If so, what does it look like?* You bet I do—and I'm happy to describe it! Mine is a photographic collage of "wish list" items that all convey the vision of me ultimately becoming a financially successful, internationally established multimedia personality who helps others. (Yes, it's highfalutin—as yours should be!) I have pictures of a fancy mansion; a Bentley; a private jet; a super yacht; and a ticket from my appearance on Oprah's radio show. Recently, I added a mock-up cover of this book with the words "*New York Times* bestseller!" on it. There is no reason in the world that you can't add to your vision board as you go forward.

I have developed the following foolproof rules for creating a vision board:

1. Never limit yourself. Don't decide you are not smart enough, too old, or any other such self-defeating idea. Believe that you are an unlimited being, receiving from an unlimited source.
2. When you make your selections, do not concern yourself with how you manifest it. (Be patient—we will cover *manifesting* soon enough!) Doing so will ruin the magic. Leave that part up to the universe, which will figure out how to make it happen. Be open to the opportunity when it comes. You'll know. Take action.

3. Whenever you look at your vision board, do not think about how nice it will be when you have the things on it. Instead, know that you *already have them*. Feel the joy of having them. This feeling is a big part of making the magic work.
4. Follow your heart. Let love decide which items you choose. Don't choose things because they are popular or because they will impress someone else. Develop your own "secret sauce" to life that works for you. You and your path are one. What you love is your path.
5. When your vision board is complete, ask yourself what actions you can take now to manifest your dreams into becoming reality. Look at all of the ways you can "lay down the red carpet" for your dreams to arrive upon.

What do you suppose Tiffany's vision board looks like? You guessed it: a chain of beauty salons; beautiful and glamorous female guests; and superstar makeup artists such as Tati Westbrook and Scott Barnes.

My eyes widened at the last item: a pair of engagement rings.

Tiffany envisioned a life not only as a successful makeup artist and entrepreneur but also as a married woman. Why not? She deserves a happy relationship, too!

Manifesting—Make It Happen

Some people think of *manifesting* in terms of some kind of New Age hocus-pocus. I can assure you it is not. Many of the most famous, intelligent, wealthy, and creative people have manifested their visions prior to them becoming reality. Comedian/actor Jim Carrey did it (signing a hefty check to himself before he "made it" in Hollywood), as did motivational speaker and *Chicken Soup for the Soul* creator Jack Canfield.

The secret is that if you truly believe in your vision, all of the thoughts and images you project become part of the outer universe. In turn, they come back to you as you conceived them.

Simplified, this is the law of attraction in motion. Your positive and negative thoughts will always come back to you. If you think positive thoughts, positive things will happen; if you think negative thoughts, negative things will happen. The good news is that you have control over your thoughts and actions and what you put out into the world.

I urge you: at all times, steer clear of negative thoughts and focus on your vision board!

There are myriad ways to use your vision board to manifest the end of your motion picture. Certainly, just looking at it throughout the day can accomplish this. You can also photograph or scan it and alternate it with your vision as your screensaver.

Another interesting way to manifest is by creating a time capsule of images and/or objects, emblazoning them in your memory, and burying them in a safe (and memorable) spot for one year. Every day until the end of the year, you must visualize the time capsule objects in your mind. One year later, you open the time capsule to see what came to fruition and what didn't. You likely will be amazed to discover that the ones that materialized were the ones you concentrated on the hardest in the most positive manner possible.

Goal Setting Leads to Results

You've come far in the second phase of the regime by creating a purpose, a mission, and a vision statement. You have a vision board and are manifesting on a regular basis. Now the rubber meets the road and serious action must be taken.

Tiffany, for example, couldn't just visualize and snap her fingers to make her dream come true. As I stressed from the beginning, there is a lot of work that must be done to progress from step A to B to C.

During the final weeks of Tiffany's stay with me, we focused on creating daily goals that worked harmoniously with her purpose and mission and would serve as stepping-stones toward fulfilling her vision. Tiffany had innate talent for makeup and hairdressing but that wasn't going to land her a job or win customers. She had to put in the time learning the trade, which meant many things had to be done up front. In order to accomplish this, we broke everything down into manageable steps.

First and foremost, Tiffany needed to find a way to pay her bills other than working as a call girl. The easiest way to accomplish this was by getting a job as a waitress. She had done it in the past and knew it was hard work for a lot less money than she was accustomed, but she was willing to do it in order to subsidize her dream.

At the same time, Tiffany attended cosmetology school and learned the trade from the ground up. She was well aware that the state of Nevada requires certification in order to be a legal practitioner. She conducted online research and found that the state required 373 days of experience. Her goal list included the following:

1. Get a waitressing job (or something similar with flexible hours).
2. Enroll in a reputable cosmetology school.
3. Set up a daily schedule blending work and training.
4. Purchase the best professional-grade tools of the trade: hairdryer, scissors, brushes, tools, tweezers, glue, mascara, lipstick, eyeliner, etcetera.
5. Find friends and classmates who would be willing to serve as practice subjects.
6. Create a portfolio of work.
7. Accept menial temp jobs at salons to gain on-the-job experience and learn from the owners and network.

After four months, Tiffany was thrilled with her new identity and ready to return to Las Vegas. She knew she had her work cut out for her but was determined to succeed. Our eyes filled with tears as she loaded up her car. We hugged and said our good-byes.

"You've done so much for me. I don't know how to thank you," she said.

"Don't thank me, thank yourself. You did all of the work and made all of your own decisions," I praised her. "The regime just pointed you in the right direction."

"Looks like I'm on my own now," she said.

"No, you aren't," I contradicted her. "You are *never* alone. You can call me anytime and I'll be there for you."

"Yes, but . . . I meant alone in Vegas."

"You have one more goal to add to your list, Tiffany: find a mentor."

"A mentor?"

"Yes," I replied. "Not a fun aunt like me—someone in the field. Someone who will take you under her wing and teach you the ropes and insider tips. *Everyone* needs a mentor at some point in her life."

"Got it," she nodded. "I'll make you proud, Clarissa."

Dominating Your Daily Demons

In order to battle your daily demons, you need to have an experienced warrior on your side: someone who can offer advice, cheer you up, give you a pep talk, or just listen whenever the negative voices start jabbering in your head. The right mentor will root for you, no matter what! We explore finding and working with a mentor and coach—as well as the distinctions between the two—in greater detail in chapter 5, Nora's story.

"You already have."

Armed with a purpose, a mission, vision board, and goals—the crucial blocks for her rebuilding program—Tiffany sped off on her journey. A few years have passed since then, during which time we have remained in frequent contact. I was genuinely touched when she sent me a lovely Mother's Day card one year later. Imagine—I had been promoted from "fun aunt" to "honorary mom"!

Since then, I have continued to offer support and positive affirmations as needed. She's had her share of successes and failures but stayed the course, thanks to the tools she had at her disposal. She waitressed, she studied, she trained, she practiced, she interned, she assisted. In short: she paid her dues and then some.

Through diligence, determination, and lots of sweat, she earned her cosmetology certificate and became a full-time makeup artist and hairdresser. But that isn't all. She met and married the man of her dreams, who loves her unconditionally and accepts her past without judgment. Ultimately, he supported her while she built her first salon—and then her second.

Tiffany is well on her way. I do not doubt for one second that someday she will have it all: a chain of salons, a horde of celebrity clientele . . . and maybe even a gaggle of children. She brims with self-esteem after utilizing only the first two stages of the regime. As we know, however, this isn't the case for everyone, as each person's circumstances differ. Tiffany is a rarity in the sense that she didn't have an issue with responsibility, a major challenge for numerous people I have encountered over the years.

Affirmation: I Am Prosperous

I am becoming more prosperous in every way I am and every day.
I am prosperous—I always have been and I always will be.
The universe looks after me and provides everything I need.
My life is filled with love, joy, and happiness.
I am abundance; prosperity is overflowing.
Prosperity is flowing and there is an abundant supply of money in my life.
My actions will lead to prosperity and abundance.
I focus my thoughts on prosperity and abundance, always.
I attract prosperity and abundance because I focus on them.
Prosperity is around me and it's within me; abundance is around me and it's within me.

REview

- Rebuild your life by choosing not to accept labels assigned to you by others.
- Rekindle your childhood dream to remind yourself of the person you are meant to be.
- Write out your purpose, mission, and vision.
- Create a vision board to help you picture where your journey will take you.
- Itemize short- and long-term goals, which should be viewed as the stepping-stones to reaching your vision.
- Find a trusted, knowledgeable mentor to help guide you through any trials and tribulations you may face along the way.

CHAPTER THREE

~

REsponsibility

Yesterday I was clever, so I wanted to change the world. Today I am wise, so I am changing myself.

—Rumi, Persian poet and scholar

Debbie is a smart, funny, and attractive fifty-something acquaintance of mine. She's also more than just a wee bit neurotic. (Aren't we all—at least to some degree?) Debbie should be living a rewarding, peaceful life, except for one major problem: she cannot make decisions. From small choices to large ones, she endlessly deliberates, ruminates, frets, changes her mind—and then changes her mind again, starting from the beginning.

Debbie's indecisiveness has had serious consequences upon every area of her life—especially socially and professionally. She has lost job opportunities and destroyed serious relationships as a result of either flip-flopping or becoming so paralyzed with indecision that she could not react at all. She constantly regrets that she didn't get the house, the car, or even a simple everyday object of desire she truly wanted because she waited too long and missed her chance.

Debbie is always settling for something less than what she really wants, which makes her feel dissatisfied and empty. She is frustrated that other people often end up making decisions for her, whether the outcome ends up favorably for her or not. Her decision-making paralysis has left her in a

perpetual funk, impacting her ability to sleep, eat right, keep her surroundings in order, and manage her affairs.
How can the regime help Debbie?

Many people are risk averse—and with good reason! Risk can be scary and sometimes result in negative consequences. However, failure to make essential decisions—even if there are substantial potential downsides—can cause even greater negative consequences and loss of reward. President John F. Kennedy once said, "There are risks and costs to action. But they are far less than the long-range risks of comfortable reaction."

You are probably asking, "What does risk aversity have to do with the subject of this chapter—*responsibility?*"

Everything! I strongly believe that taking responsibility for one's inaction is as vital as taking responsibility for missteps caused by wrong decisions. We are all human and make mistakes. If we hadn't stumbled and fallen when we were toddlers attempting to stand up for the first time, none of us would have ever developed the ability to walk. I can't imagine where I would be today if I hadn't thrown myself out there at the beginning of my career and subjected myself to the intense scrutiny of the modeling world.

Most definitions of the word *responsibility* focus on being answerable and accountable to other people, especially in terms of leadership roles and power. If you think about it, however, your greatest initial responsibility is to *yourself*. When you are on an airplane and the flight attendant explains what to do in case of a change in cabin pressure, you are specifically told to first put on your *own* oxygen mask when it drops from the ceiling. Not your spouse's, not your child's, not your elderly parent's—*yours*. Why? Because if you don't, the change in air cabin pressure will cause you to pass out within thirty seconds—and then you will be utterly useless to others and potentially put everyone in grave danger.

Taking responsibility for yourself—your decisions, your nondecisions, and your actions—is, therefore, of prime importance for your health, well-being, relationships, prosperity, and more. It also means you have no one else to blame except yourself for your decisions—good or bad—which is the way things are supposed to be.

Control Your Destiny

Debbie, the acquaintance mentioned at the beginning of the chapter, may be wired in such a way that she is averse to risk-taking in any form. I won't psychoanalyze whether the wiring is preprogrammed in her DNA, formed by her painful experiences over the years, or a combination of both factors. Whatever the cause, the result is the same: her decision-making ability is locked in place because her need to follow her internal "rule book" and maintain the status quo is equally as strong as her ambition to achieve certain important goals. The result? Risk adversity and deadlock.

This is precisely why a whole new approach is needed. The third step of the regime, responsibility, hearkens back to our previously mentioned theme of controlling one's destiny. In Debbie's case, let's suppose she's deciding between two job offers. The first is her dream job, but it's high risk and high pressure. She believes she might fail. The second opportunity is a breeze for her and far more secure, but it's a lateral move without much room for career growth. One of two things will happen: Debbie either will wait too long to decide and jeopardize being hired for either position, or she will defer to the easier job because it's safer. Either way, she ends up miserable and stuck in place.

Now, let's look at this from an entirely different perspective. Suppose Debbie knows from the get-go that her *responsibility* is to make timely decisions that are in her best interests and are *aligned with her purpose, vision, and mission*. This greatly simplifies things, doesn't it? If the high-risk job opportunity meshes with her purpose, vision, and mission and the offer terms work for her, it's a no-brainer! The risk is worth the reward and she should accept the job right away.

Dominating Your Daily Demons

What do you do if you still can't take a big leap—even after serious deliberation and drawing the conclusion that it fits with your purpose, vision, and mission?

Your responsibility is to do *whatever you must in order to defeat this daily demon*! In this instance, write down on a piece of paper what you believe the positive impact of the risky decision will be twenty years later. Close your eyes and visualize what this looks like in your mind. Guess what? You are picturing your vision!

Next, write down what happens if you choose *not* to take the risk. Visualize what the result looks like twenty years down the road. Not a pretty picture, is it? What will you lose without having tried?

Remove the state of stuck and refuse to miss your big opportunity. If you fail, so what? It was worth the effort because you were striving to fulfill your purpose. You will always have another chance but the next time with the added knowledge of what you learned from the failure.

If, however, the position *doesn't* fit with Debbie's purpose, vision, and mission, the risk is not worth the reward and she should probably decline. Once she recognizes this, her responsibility is to immediately make that decision and move on. Careful deliberation is always important—but stalling out of fear of risk and/or failure is irresponsible and potentially damaging to oneself.

The Components of Responsibility

When asked what is meant by responsibility, people often jump straight to command of financial obligations. Undoubtedly, this is one of the main areas to keep in proper order (and I address it soon enough). Every individual should be able to manage a bank account, pay bills on time, avoid debt, maintain one's possessions (such as a house, car, etc.), and avoid choices that might drain resources and compromise security. Many of us have additional financial responsibility for one or more dependents, such as a child or an aging parent, and sometimes even a cat, dog, fish, or other pet.

In addition to money matters, did you ever consider that you also have equal responsibility for the items in the list below?

- Your time and your schedule
- Your relationships
- The way you "show up" to the world

- Your commitments to yourself—especially your purpose, vision, and mission—and to others
- Your attitudes and behaviors
- Your mind, body, and spirit

I recognize that no one is perfect. There is no way a person can be 100 percent flawless in all areas of her life at all times. That said, you have a lifelong expectation to be responsible for doing the best you possibly can in all of the aforementioned areas and attempting to improve in those that may be lacking or have gone off course (even if you aren't at fault). If you do not put in the effort, your lack of responsibility results in imbalance and long-term failure to fulfill your purpose to its greatest potential.

Let's take a closer look at these responsibilities one at a time.

Invest in Your Financial Literacy

There are a lot of people who aren't so great at math. Even though I realize that managing money is not my strong suit and far from my favorite activity, I still count it high on my list of responsibilities and carefully monitor my cash flow and payments due.

First of all, managing your money means independence. You cannot be your own person if you are financially reliant upon someone else to sustain you and pay all of your bills—especially if that individual has you attached to her purse strings and keeps you at arm's distance from knowing how much money you really have in your name.

Although it might be okay for a significant other, family member, or friend to support you, you cannot be forever indebted to and supported by that person. You may lose control over what you can purchase and even find yourself unable to distinguish what is yours from hers. Imagine what a tragic, worst-case scenario—such as that individual disappearing from your life—might look like. Would you be left without resources? Would you not know the ATM machine code for your debit card? You can never place yourself in such a vulnerable position.

Mark my words: *it is your responsibility to know where the money is and how much you have.* It is also your right. I know far too many women who were married to well-off men who supported them for years and gave them whatever they needed and wanted. It seemed easy—

comfortable. But when things went south—such as divorce or the husband went bankrupt, lost his job or, worst of all, passed away—these women were left unprotected. They had no idea what the real financial situation looked like; most of the time it was not pretty.

Clar-ion Call

If someone supports you financially, the most important thing is *awareness*. You cannot assume or expect that someone will always be there to take care of you, since you never know what will happen. If your benefactor refuses to grant you knowledge about the money, it is usually a flashing red light that something is wrong, and you should probe much deeper to find out what is really going on.

By the same token, you may have a wonderful, lucrative career and be the main breadwinner for your household. That is great, but do not take your finances for granted. Situations can change on a dime (as it were). For these reasons and many others, I cover financial matters in greater depth in chapter 7.

Honor Your Time and Schedule

Your time is precious—you should never let it slip through your fingers. When you squander time, you are generally procrastinating to avoid doing something that involves effort. If it's a chore, you'll only feel even more guilty about not having done it sooner.

We waste so much time on our mobile phones: apps, texting, social media, taking and editing photographs, site surfing, and so on. Imagine what could be accomplished if you were to cut out just one hour of phone addiction a day and replace it with an action item that contributed to achieving your vision?

Television—especially binge-watching addictive cable shows—can be another major distraction that chews up your time. Like everything else, it's fine to watch in moderation as long as you get your butt off the couch to complete chores and work on your purpose, vision, and mission. I recommend exercising caution when it comes to TV news, as it can alter your mental state—especially when the coverage focuses on politics and tragic world events!

Creating a weekly schedule and sticking to it can create a solid regimen for time management. Scheduling a regular time for exercise can be especially effective. Use whatever system works best for you: virtually on your phone (Outlook, Google Calendar); an attractive, pocket-size bound calendar you can carry around; or a monthly desk blotter. Some people prefer giant dry erase boards, so activities appear prominently and things can be switched around with ease.

Clarissa's Corner

What are we to make of to-do lists? Personally, I like them because the action of writing things down emblazons them in my memory and ensures that they remain a priority. It also feels *really good* to cross things off once they are accomplished.

On the downside, to-do lists can be overdone and ultimately waste more time than they are worth. If the list is created and progress doesn't occur on the daily tasks, it may prove to be frustrating and negatively impact self-esteem. The key is to test it out for a month and determine if you made measurable progress on the to-do list. If the same actions are still on the docket after a month, this is probably not the best method for you.

It's equally as important to make enough time for pleasurable activities, such as hobbies, shopping, or whatever else floats your boat. Your brain deserves a break every now and then; afterward, you'll discover you will perform tasks with renewed energy and clarity. I address the importance of self-care a bit later in this chapter.

Show Up Well to the World

By no means does "showing up" require going to the salon every day or spending a fortune on products. You don't need to attempt to emulate hot Hollywood stars or popular Instagram influencers. You should always look and feel like your authentic self at your best.

What "showing up well to the world" does mean, however, is that you take responsibility for how you represent yourself as soon as you step out the front door (or enter a video meeting). No matter the circumstance, you should look polished, presentable, and confident at all times—even if you are tired, upset, worried, or frustrated. People will judge you based on what they see and hear—and, yes, first impressions really do matter. You also don't know when you will run into a person again under more meaningful circumstances.

Notice that successful people always present themselves well. They show up to meetings on time and prepared. They care about their hair, makeup, clothes, facial expressions, body language, and more. Again, this is not to look flashy or glamorous, but rather to seem like they *care* about themselves and that other people matter to them. When you look and act the part—whether at work or in social situations—you will already start to feel more self-confident.

Finally, "showing up" also means being civil and polite to others. When someone compliments you, for example, always respond by saying "Thank you, I appreciate that." The worst thing is to be overtly modest or self-deprecating and protest in something like the following manner: "Are you serious? I look horrible—I've gained so much weight and hardly fit in this dress!" By reacting in this dismissive way, you are being negative about yourself *and* insulting the person who offered the compliment. Even if you doubt the other person's sincerity, your manners reflect who you are and how you feel about yourself.

Fulfill Commitments to Yourself and Others

If you are someone who consistently makes promises and falls short in terms of fulfilling them, you are sending the message that you don't care and cannot be trusted. It doesn't matter how or why your commitments haven't been kept; the failures may be unintentional yet still impact how people perceive you. After a while, whether your intentions were good or not, people lose faith in you after you've disappointed them one too many times.

We all know that one colleague at work or that one family member who chronically assures others in the following manner: "No problem, I'll have it ready for you on Friday"—and then never delivers. You cannot allow yourself to ever become that person. The negative reputation caused by unreliability is difficult to overcome. If you've fallen into a pattern like this, people already may react to you in a negative way that is harming your ability to be respected. In time, it causes fractured relationships with spouses, friends, relatives, and work associates, which translates into low self-esteem. It's better to under-promise and overdeliver, rather than the other way around.

Debbie, the woman mentioned earlier in this chapter, lost several friends over the years because her poor decision making prevented her from fulfilling certain promises to others. She wasted so much time deliberating about how to fulfill requests that she often neglected her agreed-upon deadlines and promises.

It is equally as important that you are responsible for keeping promises you make to yourself. If you set goals—especially those associated with your purpose, vision, and mission—with specific deadlines for yourself, you must ensure that you follow through on them. If you miss them, you will end up beating yourself up and making yourself feel even worse, which, of course, leads to low self-esteem.

On the other hand, it is also your responsibility to forgive yourself for disappointing yourself and others. Once you have apologized to yourself and the people you inconvenienced, you need to work even harder to regain trust, forgive yourself, and move on. Make it a point to vow that this is the last time that this will ever occur—and then deliver each and every instance after that!

Take Charge of Your Attitudes and Behaviors

If you are an introverted person who feels uncomfortable with others in social situations, you inadvertently may be sending out bad vibes to the world that you are unhappy, don't want to be there, dislike the people in your company, or you are above them in some way. Trust me: no one wants to be around someone who is pessimistic, negative, or condescending.

You are perfectly entitled to be introverted. It is your responsibility, however, to find a way to exhibit proper attitudes and behaviors so that you give others an opportunity to accept you and treat you with respect. It may sound phony to pretend like this but being socially appropriate is an *expectation* that others have of you, no matter what the circumstance. Chances are, your impressions of the people you dislike may be superficial or inaccurate, created by chatter in your head. There are times, for example, when you assume people dislike you or think you are unattractive, ignorant, poorly dressed, and so forth, when in reality they don't believe that—or aren't focusing on you at all.

Never assume what others may be thinking and always take the high road. You never know when someone you meet at a gathering can become an ally to you and help you fulfill your vision down the road. What others think of you is none of your business!

Clarissa's Corner

The keys to being responsible:

- Do what you are supposed to do.
- Plan ahead.
- Persevere.
- Always do your best.
- Exercise self-control.
- Be self-disciplined.
- Think before you act—consider the consequences.
- Be accountable for your words, actions, and attitude.
- Set a good example for others.
- Take good care of yourself!

See? I told you early on that none of my recommendations would be too radical!

Affirmation: I Am Responsible

I am responsible for creating my purpose, mission, vision, and goals.

I am responsible for striving to fulfill my purpose, mission, vision, and goals while avoiding distractions.

I am responsible for acknowledging and learning from mistakes/failures and then moving on.

I am responsible for recognizing the role I might inadvertently be playing in unhealthy relationships.

I am responsible for my own mistakes.

I am responsible for taking action and accepting necessary risks when they help fulfill my vision.

I am responsible for my financial independence.

I am responsible for being the best I can be in professional and learning scenarios.

I am responsible for nourishing my mind, body, and spirit.

I am responsible for presenting well and showing up.
I am responsible for acknowledging and improving my imperfections.
I am responsible for working to overcome my fears.
I am responsible for treating myself with kindness and respect, even when I mess up.
I am responsible for not being overly critical of others.
I am responsible for getting help and support as needed.
I am responsible for resisting being compared to others.
I am responsible for forgiving myself.
I am responsible for my own happiness.

REview

- Be responsible for making your own decisions—and living with them.
- Say "yes" to decisions that help you fulfill your vision.
- Take responsibility for how well you manage your time and schedule.
- Show up well to the world and always fulfill your commitments.

CHAPTER FOUR

~

REplace

Diplomas can't replace self-development.

—Sunday Adelaja, Ukrainian pastor

Brooke Walker has an unbelievable story. When she was eight years of age, her parents brought her into an Arizona cult. On the surface, the cult seemed like a warm, family environment filled with educated people—including Brooke's father, who was an attorney with a private practice—and its members were free to go into town and even work at jobs outside the community. Brooke attended the cult's school until she was fifteen years old, after which she worked as a receptionist in her father's legal practice.

Any semblance of normalcy ended there. Brooke did not reside with her parents and her marital arrangement was assigned to her when she was only seventeen. A medium or "trance leader" ran group sessions during which members were brainwashed and demeaned with degrading labels. Being called "worthless" was one of the least offensive words used. Families had no control over choosing their romantic partners; where they lived—sometimes they were forced to switch living situations for no apparent reason; the foods they ate; or the friendships they kept.

Fed up with the explosive infighting, constant screaming, and lack of control in her life, Brooke escaped from the cult twice with her two children.

Although the first time failed because she lacked the tools to live indepen-
dently, the second effort stuck. Brooke's overarching problem? The experi-
ences and brainwashing from the cult continued to haunt and rule her.

After divorcing her husband from the prearranged marriage, Brooke faced
the seemingly impossible task of starting anew with her family. Her children
lacked civility and were constantly getting into trouble with the law. She
struggled to discipline them, falling back on methods passed on to her from
the cult: yelling and name-calling.

Personally, she had to cope with years of psychological and emotional
abuse that led to alcoholism and cardiovascular issues.

Brooke felt broken and helpless, well aware that she had to replace her
mind-set and all of her deep-seated, self-damaging habits with healthy and
productive new ones. Unfortunately, she didn't know what "normal" life
outside the cult looked and felt like. She couldn't begin to figure out what she
was missing from her life, much less which holes needed to be filled.

I bet you have a lot of buzzing negativity in your head—some real,
some imagined, and a lot exaggerated. In order to feel confident and
successful, you must dismiss negative thinking and then replace it with
words, thoughts, and actions that instill you with power and control.
This means tuning out—and potentially replacing—the people in your
life who don't fully support you. As Mark Twain once said, "Keep away
from people who try to belittle your ambitions. Small people always do
that but the really great make you feel that you, too, can become great."

The release process I'm about to share with you is not all going to be
fun and easy. Some of this will be uncomfortable. It can be excruciat-
ingly painful to let go of people but, in the long run, you will be much
better off. The secret to making this work? Release whatever is harming
you (chapter 1); take responsibility for your actions and words (chapter
3); and replace negative people and things you've let go of with ones
that fill gaps and make you feel good.

There are endless things in your life that can potentially be replaced
and improved:

- Junk—with objects and things symbolizing a positive future
- Friends and lovers who do not support you—with people who do
- Toxic people in your life—with supportive people

- Wasted time—with productive things that fulfill your vision, purpose, mission, and goals
- A lousy job—with something more fulfilling
- Bad thoughts—with good
- Detrimental environments (i.e., rooms, including those in your home)—with inspiring ones
- An old mind-set—with a new one
- Bad habits (i.e., related to diet)—with beneficial ones

On the encouraging side, there are far fewer people, places, and things that you can't ever replace, such as the person you are deep inside and the family that raised you. In these instances, it once again becomes a case of knowing that you cannot control things that are uncontrollable—so stop worrying about them! Instead, focus on coping with them as best you can and instilling joy in other aspects of your life (which, in a sense, is still a form of replacement).

Some Unfortunate Facts

I sincerely hope you have never found yourself in an extreme situation like Brooke Walker, whose story I told at the beginning of this chapter. Unfortunately, the statistical odds indicate that most people have experienced some kind of abuse in their lifetimes. Take a moment to soak in these sobering statistics from the United States alone:

- According to the National Children's Alliance, nearly 700,000 children are abused each year.
- Statista reports that 1.2 million violent crimes occur each year.
- The National Statistics Domestic Violence Fact Sheet estimates that one in four women and one in nine men are victims of domestic violence.

Of course, these numbers reflect reported cases, so we can only presume that the actual numbers are significantly higher. I don't bring this up to frighten you or equate any of these situations with each other (or with cults) except to say that, given such prevalence of these issues, odds are that you have experienced some form of abuse or know a person who has. It may be some consolation to you that at least you are not alone, although sometimes it may feel that way.

No matter the circumstances, abuse almost always leads to low self-esteem. Even if you have completed the first three stages of this regime, there inevitably will be residual lingering bad memories and feelings remaining from past traumas—even if you have had some form of therapy. Like Brooke, you may be in a situation in which you are so confused about what needs replacing in your life that you don't even know where to begin. Brooke had to start completely from scratch and replace pretty much everything in her life (especially people): her love life; her family; her friends; her physical home; her professional life; her manner of interacting with others; her parenting skills; the foods she ate; the care of her body; and, most of all, the programmed thoughts in her head.

The good news is that Brooke has been successfully conquering her demons and replacing all of the above with improvements across the board. In the years subsequent to her second escape from the cult, she has stopped drinking; taken better care of her diet and body through proper nutrition and exercise; moved into a new home; separated from the cult; became closer than ever with her children; made new friends; and earned a degree in psychology. She is striving toward accomplishing a unique mission that connects her legal background (working with her father) to her knowledge of psychology: creating a program that helps attorneys overcome stress.

Brooke rose up, making brave decisions that changed the course of her life for herself and her family. If she was capable of replacing the things that were harmful to her, you can, too!

Table 4.1. Things You Can and Can't Replace

Can't Replace	Can Replace
Good friends	Friends who make you feel lousy
Family	Time spent with family members who hurt you
The person you are meant to be	Being cruel to another person
Your true purpose	A job and/or a career
True love	A bad relationship
Negative thoughts when they aren't replaced by positive ones	Negative thoughts
Lost time	How you will spend your time in the future
Failure to try	Past failure with a new attempt

Replacing Your Words

When we make a mistake—such as accidentally slicing a finger while chopping carrots—what's the first thing we typically say (after "Ouch!" of course)? "Stupid, stupid, stupid!" That's right. We blame *ourselves*, as if the pain of cutting a finger isn't enough damage and punishment.

Negative words can inflict an enormous amount of harm on your psyche—especially when they are self-generated in your head. In a sense, your personal inner voice—which is really just noise—turns you into your worst enemy. I bet many things you think or say aloud about yourself are far worse than anything said to you by people who were angry at you or who simply didn't like you.

Dominating Your Daily Demons

What people, places, or things need replacement in your life?

In your journal or on a separate sheet of paper, list ten things you need to remove from your life and ten things you might replace them with. These shouldn't be just any old worn-out possessions (such as a beat-up car with 200,000 miles on it), but rather things that make you feel like you've hit a dead end. They might be things such as finding a new romantic partner or friend; exploring an exciting career path; or discovering a new hobby. Although you can't really replace family members, you can decide which of these may require a bit of separation and distance.

Equally as important, on your list of ten items, be sure to also include negative thoughts, words, behaviors, and actions that need to be replaced. Remember the law of attraction: positive or negative thoughts bring positive or negative experiences into a person's life.

Try to do at least three things every week that bring you closer to obtaining the desired items on your list. If you succeed at only one of the ten per month, you will be able to resolve the entire list in less than a year!

Self-harming internal language must *always* be replaced. It's one thing to release negative words and phrases such as *I can't*, but what happens if you don't subsequently substitute them with something empowering? They end up being replaced by different negative words.

Below are some easy-to-remember positive replacement phrases for the negative ones. Anytime you find yourself starting a sentence with the phrases below—whether thinking it or saying it aloud—check yourself right away and reword it as specified.

Original: I *can't pass* the test.
Replacement: *I will pass the test if I work hard and study.*

Original: I *could never run* as fast as Darci.
Replacement: *Darci is a great runner, but I have my own goals to reach.*

Original: *Is it possible* I'll get the manager position someday?
Replacement: *It's entirely possible I'll become manager someday.*

Original: It *won't* ever happen.
Replacement: *It could happen.*

Original: I *don't belong* in the top class in school.
Replacement: *I'm already in the top class in school, so I must belong here.*

Original: I'm *not good enough to be accepted* into an Ivy League school.
Replacement: *I am more than smart enough to be accepted into an Ivy League school.*

Original: I *don't deserve* this promotion.
Replacement: *I worked hard for this promotion and I deserve it.*

Original: Why do I *always screw things up?*
Replacement: *I always learn from my mistakes and do much better the next time around.*

If you ever feel negative thoughts and emotions swirling in your head and can't find replacements along the lines of those suggested above, jot down in your notebook (or on a separate sheet of paper) five of your strongest attributes *and* five things you have successfully accomplished that week. Read these ten items to yourself and then convincingly say them out loud. Repeat this exercise until the negative thoughts have been replaced by those you've written down.

Ditch the Labels

At the beginning of this chapter, I recounted how the word "worthless" was used by cult leaders to demean and brainwash Brooke and others in the cult. Whether or not you were subjected to this type of verbal and psychological abuse, insults of all kinds have a way of lingering in your mind and festering. If unreplaced, they become labels sewn deep into your psyche. Childhood taunts about weight, hair, nose, braces, fashion sense, and other visual aspects of our younger selves often sting us, even if we have long outgrown those traits—although, more likely, they were never true in the first place.

In the introduction of this book, I described how I felt like an "ugly duckling" as a child. That label might have permanently stuck—and I never would have explored modeling and acting—had I not ultimately replaced those two words with "swan."

You, too, may be a late bloomer. Others may not see your inner and outer beauty only because you have been holding on to worn-out labels and haven't replaced them with accurate, up-to-date, favorable ones. Elle Macpherson—one of the most beautiful women on the planet—had a similar experience. She described it to a magazine reporter: "I was six feet tall at eighteen and now think of the time I wasted wishing I was smaller. I had all those insecure feelings about a big nose, big ears, and being too tall. . . . That awkwardness was there all the time. I never looked at myself and thought that I was a swan. All I could see was an ugly duckling."

Consider these stunning actresses and models who overcame childhood labels to reach the pinnacle of success:

- Tyra Banks thought she was a "chubby girl" before having a growth spurt—and then believed she had become "sick and frail."
- Nicole Kidman considered herself "gangly."
- Jennifer Garner regarded herself as a "geek."
- Salma Hayek had severe teenage acne that she labeled a "deformity."
- Jessica Alba saw herself as "pigeon-toed," "cross-eyed," and bucktoothed."
- Lucy Liu was picked on because she was a "toothpick."

• Jennifer Aniston, like Elle and me, also thought of herself as an "ugly duckling."

Do you notice a recurring trend in these examples? Looking at all of these gorgeous women today, it's hard to believe they ever accepted such terrible labels as fact. Yet this was clearly the case. Trust me when I say they weren't displaying false modesty to make themselves seem relatable. Certainly, some of the concerns these superstars had with their appearance when they were younger (such as acne) dissipated with time.

More often than not, however, negative labels tend to have greater unconscious impact on us than we realize—especially if they originated from the negative messaging of others. The people who are most successful ditch the labels and use them to their advantage. Perhaps the labels forced upon them provided extra motivation for them to attain their goals.

Some go as far as flipping the story by turning the negative label into an identifiable brand. For example, what do Sarah Jessica Parker, Barbra Streisand, Maya Rudolph, Mayim Bialik, and Meryl Streep have in common? Some might answer that they all have "big noses." Toss that away! I would instead propose that they are talented actresses with *beautiful trademark* looks.

Clar-ion Call

No matter how well-intentioned, affectionate, and caring your friends and relatives might seem to be, you cannot allow them to continue to use negative labels that originated during your childhood. Expressions (and possibly nicknames) as simple as "four eyes," "pizza face," or "nerd" that may no longer even be true can continue to stir up terrible childhood memories.

You will not have a chance to ditch and replace the labels if other people in your life continue to dredge them up out of playfulness or nostalgia. Tribe mentality will always hold you down and keep you in the pattern and in that role. If you are the clown in the group, the other members will continue to figuratively smash pies in your face.

When this occurs, you must speak up. You can say something along the lines of "Hey, I know you don't mean it, but can you please stop calling me that? I hated it back and then and I hate it even more now."

If the friend insists on calling you such things after you have made a sincere request, it's time to ditch and replace her. If it's a relative, be polite as needed but replace the time spent with her in favor of being with another relative who reinforces the things that make you feel good.

Recognize this fact: *it's a privilege to be in your company—it must be earned!*

Mirror, Mirror

Mirror affirmations can be a truly impactful technique for replacing negative beliefs with positive ones. The concept was initially popularized by the late Louise Hay—a motivational speaker, author, and book publisher who referred to it as "mirror work" (perhaps to distinguish it from "mirror therapy," which is an entirely different treatment). Hay believed that by reciting and repeating certain statements (affirmations) while looking at your reflection in the mirror, it is possible to rewire your subconscious to think more confidently and enable the positive messages to become habitual and second nature.

I have developed a specific methodology for a mirror affirmation process that is effective for replacing bad thoughts in your head. It takes twenty-one days to complete and requires close adherence to the directions, but trust me—it's well worth it! A side benefit of mirror affirmations is that you have an excuse to talk to yourself without anyone thinking you are going crazy!

Be prepared: this technique is powerful and may stir up many emotions. I encourage you to plow through it and feel all of the sensations that materialize. At first, you may also feel a tad silly, but I promise you will start to notice improvements in your mind-set after just the first couple of days.

You should recite the affirmations at least twice a day, preferably when you wake up and again before you go to sleep. If you have time during the day, you can add extra sessions; the more, the better!

Step 1: Find a mirror on the wall, preferably one that is full-sized to reflect your entire body. (If this isn't possible, you can still continue with a smaller one.)

Step 2: Choose one of the affirmation lines from the list below:

You are confident.
You respect yourself.
You are awesome.
You are not what others think of you.
You were created for greatness.
You inspire others.
You are a leader.
You are growing as a person every day.
You are proud of yourself.
You will not settle for less than you deserve.
You are good to yourself.
You are smart.
You are fun to be around.
You are worthy.
You take care of yourself and your body.
You are capable of handling anything.
You believe in yourself.
You are beautiful.
You are secure in yourself and who you are.
It is safe and okay for you to love yourself.

Step 3: Standing in front of the mirror, take three long, deep breaths. If you are someone who is impatient and rushes through things, count to three on the breath in and three on the breath out.

Step 4: Without taking your eyes off your reflection, slowly state your affirmation ten times while addressing yourself as "you" (not "I"). Be certain you are fully experiencing the sentiment of the statement each time you recite it.

Step 5: Observe how you feel afterward. Are the negative thoughts still in your head? Or have they been replaced by the words you said in front of the mirror?

Step 6: Write down your free-flowing thoughts in your journal immediately afterward.

You can choose a different affirmation if the one you selected doesn't
seem to have enough punch to knock out the negative thoughts. You
may also alternate between two affirmations, if you like, but do not add
more than that, as it might dilute your self-messaging.

Clarissa's Corner

Everyone has a bad day every now and then—it's okay! When this
happens, you may want to employ a mirror mind trick to prevent
the day's events from seeping into the progress you've made during
the twenty-one-day mirror affirmation process.

While standing in front of the mirror and looking at your reflection, shout the following, out loud, ten times: "Today totally
sucked—tomorrow will be better!"

Yes, I know it sounds a bit cliché—like Little Orphan Annie
singing "Tomorrow" or Scarlett O'Hara proclaiming, "Tomorrow
is another day!" at the end of Gone with the Wind—but it can put
you back on track and improve your mood by blaming "the day" for
your problems instead of yourself.

It's perfectly fine if you can't control laughing your way through
this. At the least, you are bringing yourself out of the doldrums and
into a happier frame of mind.

After twenty-one days, do a self-check to observe any changes and
improvements. Flip back the pages in your journal to review days one
to twenty-one. Is your writing gradually becoming more positive from
one day to the next? During the day, do you find yourself hearing your
voice reciting the mirror affirmation? Perhaps you even picture your
face and body language in your mind while recalling it.

Affirmation: The Envelopment Pledge

I [Insert your name here], *hereby declare to:*
Invest in my personal envelopment in wise and beneficial ways.
Be responsible for my health, well-being, wealth, fitness, and happiness.

Embrace my life's vision with purpose and passion.
Never compare myself to others, as everyone's journey is unique.
Understand that I already have everything that I need.
Treat myself like I'm my own best friend.
Be in the right place at the right time with the right attitude.
Give and receive easily.
Add value to people's lives.
Be positively powerful.
Be a bold, confident, and visible leader.
Get rid of thoughts that aren't useful, beautiful, or joyful.
Not take myself so seriously.
Dream more while I'm awake.
See myself as beautiful just the way I am.
Know that I matter.
Know that I am loved.
Know that I make a difference.
Understand that I am not entitled and the world owes me nothing.
Recognize that I owe it to myself and to the world to live the greater good.
Know that whatever does or doesn't happen, I am enough—just the way I am.

REview

- Recognize and accept that all negative thoughts, feelings, people, places, and things can be replaced with something better.
- Identify what you must replace in your life—even when it might be challenging to do so.
- Replace negative words such as "I can't" with positive spins, such as "I will."
- Ditch the old labels that have stuck to you and substitute them with positive attributes.
- Try the mirror affirmation process for twenty-one days and detail the gradual improvement in your journal.

CHAPTER FIVE

~

REaffirm

Act as if what you do makes a difference. It does.

—William James, psychologist and philosopher

Let's try something different for this chapter. Rather than begin with a profile of someone who struggled with and overcame an aspect of self-esteem, I would like to introduce someone who embodies the fifth stage of the regime, reaffirm: Nora Gay.

Nora is one of the most remarkable women I have ever encountered: a brilliant and strong self-made success. Born and raised in Haiti, she graduated from Harvard University, where she studied law. Later, she earned her master's in finance from Boston University. Now a financial strategist, entrepreneur, and author of the book Get Minted!*, she represents the pinnacle of accomplishment.*

How has she made it this far? By staying true to herself and her heritage. Having recognized the gap in financial literacy in her own family amid turbulent socioeconomic and political times in Haiti, she went on a mission to bring her knowledge back to the Haitian community and improve the quality of life for as many women as possible.

Her journey began when the husband of a close friend passed away from colon cancer. Her widowed friend, left with virtually nothing while raising their eleven-month-old child, was one step away from living in the streets. Not only did Nora help her friend get through this difficult time by offering solid financial planning advice, she sought to ensure this situation didn't happen to others.

As Nora explains, "Haiti is a complex place for women. The social life there can be chaotic. My goal is do my part to organize the chaos. Financial literacy and stability are so important to self-confidence and empowering women."

Nora tapped her heritage as she set about helping women create better environments for themselves. She recognizes the importance of finance in helping to empower women, especially when they are young. By reaffirming her own identity through her culture, education, and personal experiences and then reflecting them outward to help others, she has firmly established her remarkable place in the world.

It goes without saying that Nora put her vast knowledge and skills to good use. Did she always have an easy ride along the way? Certainly not. Early on, she was self-aware enough to identify important areas that needed improvement and/or strengthening.

The one thing Nora did *not* do was beat herself up for her normal human imperfections. She recognized that none of us is perfect; we all have skills, talents, and behaviors that could stand some personal and professional growth. Recognizing this and then doing something proactive about it became an essential part of her plan. At the same time, she needed to find a way to reaffirm her strengths and remain self-confident about herself and everything she had to share with the world.

Let's explore what Nora did.

Put Me in, Coach!

We all have a range of strengths and weaknesses. We also have the means within ourselves to improve the latter—at least up to a point. No matter how successful we may be, there is always room *to be better.* A strong, self-confident person admits to this fact even if she has already come a long way through the first four phases of this regime. But how is it possible for a person to be objective about areas in need of improvement? This can be painful and, if not handled properly, can lead to decreased self-esteem.

This is why it's so crucial to find someone who can work with you on your development and growth while also edifying you and reaffirming your greatness. To cut to the chase: you can live up to your fullest potential by finding a suitable coach.

There is no shame in working with a coach. Nora had a coach. I've been coached over the years. And notables such as Bill Clinton, Oprah Winfrey, Bill Gates, Eric Schmidt, Sheryl Sandberg, and Steve Jobs all had coaches at one time or another.

Choosing between a Mentor and a Coach

Although the terms *mentor* and *coach* overlap to some degree, they are not interchangeable. Some professionals have their own distinctions between the two, but I see it this way:

- A mentor is an experienced, trusted adviser who helps a trainee learn, progress, or improve in a company—sometimes targeting specific work skills and behaviors.
- A coach is a trained professional who usually performs this role exclusively and utilizes creative means to help an individual fulfill his or her fullest potential in life and/or in business.

How do you determine which one you need? Nora had a two-in-one scenario: her informal work mentor had been so helpful to her that she later hired him as her personal coach.

A mentor is often someone within your company who knows the ropes and can help you succeed in that specific organization. Sometimes companies have mentoring programs designed for such a purpose and assign all new employees mentors. (There are also more modern organizations that think "mentor" sounds old-fashioned, corny, and/or condescending, so they may prefer to use the term *adviser* or the less formal *buddy*.) In other cases, an executive may choose to take someone under his or her wing and provide casual mentoring that both parties feel provides the most tangible value.

Chances are, if you have had any kind of self-esteem issues and are looking to improve your personal and professional life, getting a coach (sometimes referred to as a "life coach") is the way to go. Unfortunately, since coaches worth their salt can be pricey, companies tend to limit offering their services only to senior executives and perhaps those employees that they feel are raw talent that can be groomed. If you don't fall into either of those categories, you must take matters into your own hands to maximize your abilities, to feel good about yourself, to get ahead, and to realize your vision, mission, and purpose.

Criteria for Choosing a Coach

As much as your budget allows—even if only for just a session or two—I advise hiring the perfect life coach *for you*. Note the emphasis on those last two words. Anyone can hang up a shingle (or build a website) and call herself a "life coach," so let's get specific in terms of how to choose the right professional and set expectations with her.

1. *Highly regarded*: The coach comes recommended from people you admire and respect. Word of mouth is always a great place to start.
2. *Natural rapport*: You want to choose a coach with whom conversations are natural and smooth. Although the coach isn't your therapist, the roles are similar in that a certain level of comfort is required.
3. *Trustworthy*: Your coach isn't a physician or an attorney, but you still need to be certain everything you say is kept confidential. You also need to be certain that the information she provides to you is trustworthy and accurate.
4. *Focused*: Pick a coach who is thoughtful, organized, and keeps her attention strictly *on you* during sessions. You don't want someone who is easily distracted.
5. *Relatable*: The coach needs to be someone you identify with, meaning you appreciate her manner and style and look up to her.
6. *Empathetic*: The coach must demonstrate that she understands who you are and what you've been through. She has the where-

withal to empathize with you and whatever situation or crisis you are facing. She is always on your side, cheering you on with unconditional support.

7. *X-ray vision:* The coach should be someone who is able to see *right through you.* No, I don't mean that the coach become super personal! (In fact, to the contrary, there should be some careful boundaries in place.) Rather, the coach needs to possess the ability to see you objectively and reflect things back to you that you don't see in yourself. Some of us—including me—put walls (defense mechanisms) around us that prevent others from seeing inside; a good coach can use her X-ray vision to break through them and get right inside your head.

8. *Honesty:* This one is tricky. Your coach should be able to give it to you straight without denigrating you. Any whiff of negativity or condescension will send you right back to square one. That said, the coach sometimes needs to give you tough love to sensitively tell you when something requires extra attention.

Nora offers some helpful attributes to add to the list above when she seeks a coach: "I want to believe the coach has an innate gift to do what he or she does. Also, he or she can provide wisdom, insights, and a new perspective. Someone who can reaffirm your greatness as well as work with you on things for development."

Dominating Your Daily Demons

I can't drive this point home enough: it's perfectly okay to get a coach! Although no one has to even know that you have one, there isn't any stigma associated with it. It's not psychotherapy (although there is nothing wrong with that, either). In your mind, do not allow yourself to think that there is something wrong with you for seeking out a coach to help you with personal growth and development and to provide a reaffirming viewpoint that will make you feel strong and confident. Think of it like you are getting an extra shot of adrenaline before facing the outside world!

The Coaching Process

There isn't necessarily a right or wrong methodology when it comes to life coaching. You just want to be sure that it's a good fit and in sync with helping you accomplish your goals. In Nora's case, her coach helped her to identify and work on a couple of personal challenges: overanalyzing things and overworking herself. For the latter, her coach helped her realize that she was racing to get everything done, which tired her out. The coach enabled her to reassess her work as a "marathon and not a sprint." This did the trick, slowing her down to the right working speed while still getting her tasks done on time, if not early. Best yet, she blew her goals out of the water! It felt good for Nora to share in her accomplishments with her coach, who lavished praise on her.

Clar-ion Call

As I've mentioned, there are myriad excellent tools—that is, behavioral surveys—available to coaches. Some prefer to stick with only one, whereas others may be willing to work with you on whichever one you trust (as long as it isn't your astrological sign).

These are just a few commonly used assessments:

- *StrengthsFinder*: Based on the theories of Don Clifton and adapted to book format (as *StrengthsFinder 2.0*) by Gallup, this is a positive approach to determining a person's gifts and focusing on them rather than weaknesses. This one works particularly well for reaffirming self-confidence.
- *Enneagram*: A system that helps identify how a person sees the world and manages her emotions.
- *Myers-Briggs*: A questionnaire that identifies how an individual perceives the world and makes decisions based on her preferences. This involves much more than identifying whether you are an introvert versus an extrovert (which you probably already figured out on your own).

Reaffirming Who You Are

For whatever reason—but especially personal experience—you may continue to be disenchanted by something connected to your cultural background, heritage, race, religion, or family history. Although you released your baggage associated with it back in chapter 1, you may still be able to tap into a positive aspect or two of these areas that could reaffirm your self-esteem. You may not ever fully be able to fully embrace your roots—nor do I suggest that this is essential—but it's worth investigating to determine what gold nuggets can be mined to help foster your personal growth and development.

Nora, for example, successfully blended her analytical skills, education, and financial capabilities with her love for her fellow Haitians and by identifying an area where she could be of service. By reaffirming this as a source of strength, she was able to look past the chaos of the socioeconomic and political conditions there and recognize how she could benefit her people. In her mind, financial literacy empowers women and instills self-confidence and leads to ultimate success. Her purpose, therefore, centered around digging deep within herself to give something of herself to help others.

Clarissa's Corner

What submerged part of your past can you potentially reaffirm in some way to benefit yourself and other people? Again, I want to emphasize that you don't need to become evangelical, if you somehow feel estranged from the religion you were born into. However, if your family was devoutly Christian, perhaps there is *one aspect* of the religion you can reaffirm, such as performing charity work. Volunteering at a church food drive, for example, could be a good way to reaffirm your Christian upbringing and feel proud that this is part of you.

Reaffirming Your Self-Esteem with the Four E's

Mary L. Holden, an editor and writer friend based in Phoenix, Arizona, loves etymology and playing with words. She offers a unique take on the hidden layers of meaning behind words, which she refers to as *ontological semiosis*. It happens that she has taken a deep dive into the significance of what is embedded within the hyphenated word *self-esteem*.

If you'll note, *self-esteem* has four *e*'s in it, which is unusual, to say the least. (I bet you can't think of one that is similar, except for maybe *cheesesteak*!) Mary associates meaning with each letter *e* in the word, as follows:

- *Electricity:* Always present in the human body, electrical power is the result of resistance. People need to learn how to make this foundation of natural resistance work well for them on the emotional layer.
- *Energy:* Identifying your level of energy is important—but how do you figure this out? You can do it using Myers-Briggs or a similar personality assessment tool.
- *Expansion:* People do not go up or down or side-to-side in terms of personal growth, but rather inward and outward. In order to truly expand oneself in all directions, outward expansion is the best way to understand personal growth in this era of human evolution.
- *Ease:* There is a tendency for humans to make things more difficult than they need to be. Simplification is the best way to get through your day, avoid problems, and reach greater heights of accomplishment.

Let's break these out one at a time. . . .

Tapping into Your Electricity

Although I would never want to be on the receiving end of a lightning bolt, the human body bursts with electrical energy. At all times, our brains require electricity to send signals back and forth to and from our nervous system in order for us to think, act/react, and sense things.

When a heart stops, a life-saving technique known as defibrillation is performed, in which pads placed on the chest send electrical currents to shock the heart back to life. The natural chemicals in our bodies—sodium, calcium, potassium, and magnesium, for example—all contain an electrical charge.

How do we tap into such powerful electricity without becoming Frankenstein or a burnt spot on the ground? It's actually simple science: *be active—go for a walk or ride a bicycle.*

Many science museums have exhibits in which visitors can take turns riding a stationary bicycle that is wired to a light bulb. The faster you pedal, the brighter the bulb glows. The same is true internally as well. Something as simple as riding a bike stimulates electricity throughout the body and in the brain that helps you feel more powerful and alert, which raises feelings of self-esteem.

If you want to reaffirm the electrical currents in your body, a fifteen-minute walk or bike ride could be just the answer you have been seeking.

Connecting with Your Internal Energy

The theory goes that energy cannot be created nor destroyed. That may be true, but that doesn't mean we don't have the power to boost energy that already exists in our bodies.

Human beings consist of billions of molecules—most of them water-based—that are constantly in motion. Even while at rest, a human body produces 100 watts of power. When performing strenuous exercise, an individual is capable of producing up to 2,000 watts of energy—most of which ends up getting wasted.

How can we tap into and benefit from our internal energy? In one of her wonderful motivational speeches, best-selling author and the writer of the foreword of this book Sharon Lechter (*Think and Grow Rich for Women*, among many others) prompts her audience—men and women alike—to stand up tall and pose like the comic book character Wonder Woman: legs apart and hands at the hips while pushing out the chest and breathing deeply in and out. If you hold this pose for a mere twenty seconds, you reaffirm the natural energy and power in your body and feel enormously confident.

Best of all, you can do this any time of day!

Expanding Your Horizons

If we were to stay in one position too long, our muscles would begin to feel tight and may even cramp and/or atrophy. If we were to stay indoors too long, we likely would feel suffocated and perhaps suffer from a shortage of sunlight, which provides vitamin D. If we were to do the same routine every day, we would get bored and listless. To summarize: we can't possibly hope to expand ourselves if we rely solely on inward energy.

How do we expand our horizons to just the right amount? As much as safety allows, you must get out in the world: travel; find a hobby; participate in a community project; go to fairs, festivals, carnivals, amusement parks, and recreational parks; join a club; and so forth. In order to reaffirm yourself as the person you are destined to become, you must also reaffirm with the world itself. For our purposes, let's adapt the line from John Donne's famous poem for our times (my changes are in italics): "No *one* is an island. Every *person* is a piece of the continent, a part of the main; if a clod be washed away by the sea, *every individual* is a piece of the continent, a part of the main."

By the way, the word *clod* does not refer to a stupid person. Rather, it means a lump of earth or clay. We—human beings, that is—are lumps of clay that connect everywhere in the world to everyone through water and earth. We can mold ourselves into whatever form we choose!

Easy Peasy

Another major lesson we can glean from Nora's reaffirming experiences is the *ease* by which she goes about her life and business. She identifies a problem that she or a community of people face and then seeks to solve it head on. This is where her analytical skills truly shine! She derives confidence from her strengths—and you should, too, no matter what they might be.

When problems arise, emotional feelings and behaviors tend to surface and get in the way. We crawl within ourselves out of fear or lash out with aggressive anger known as "cave brain." (If you are looking for an excellent book on the subject, check out Daniel Goleman's classic *Emotional Intelligence*.) Although it's a good thing to be human and *feel*, there is also a time when you just need to turn off that emotional spigot to problem-solve and get the job done.

We all overcomplicate our daily lives in some fashion. We overstuff our closets, save things we don't need, sign up for too many email lists, post too many selfies, and so forth and then wonder why we are overwhelmed, can't focus, and never seem to have enough time. The best way for you to overcome this perpetual situation is to reaffirm in your journal the things that are most meaningful and impactful to you:

1. My *relationships*: Focus on your lover/significant other, friends, coworkers, community members, pet, and so on.
2. My *vision, mission, and purpose*: Check out your vision board and work toward making this happen!
3. My *body*: Exercise and eat right.
4. My *mind*: Stimulate your mind with productive hobbies, such as puzzles and books.

Note: Social media interactions won't fill your bucket like the above four areas will. I'm not suggesting shutting it down entirely—but setting careful time limits on scrolling and posting will reward you with hundreds of extra hours in a year. If you are on Facebook or Instagram more than a half hour per day, you are overcomplicating your life. By cutting back just a bit every day and using that time to read, for example, imagine how many novels you could complete in a year. Better yet, maybe you could finally make time for writing your own work of fiction!

What will *you* vow to do to make your life easier?

Affirmation: Today

Today I will reaffirm an aspect of my proud heritage.
Today I reaffirm what I will and will not accept as truth.
Today I reaffirm that only healthy uplifting relationships will be a part of my life.
Today I reaffirm that I will uplift others with caring, kindness, and benevolence.
Today I reaffirm my undying belief that I am enough.
Today I affirm my undying love for myself.

REview

- Hire a coach to help you reaffirm your strengths.
- When selecting a coach, find someone you trust who is highly regarded, provides you with honest feedback, makes you feel accomplished, and fully "gets" you.
- Reaffirm one positive aspect of your neglected past—which may be related to your faith, ethnicity, community, family, and so forth—that may be of value to you and others today.
- Tap into the four e's of self-esteem: electricity, energy, expansion, and ease.

CHAPTER SIX

~

REinvent

There's nothing more addictive or incredible in life than reinventing yourself and allow[ing] yourself to be different every day.

—Thalia, Mexican singer and songwriter

*Lisa has worked the same job for eight years. She doesn't love it or hate it.
It's helped pay the bills, and the company accommodates her flexible schedule
as she and her husband raise their two young children.*

*Lisa has received mediocre reviews from her supervisor each year, accom-
panied by the company's average 2 percent annual salary increase. She has
remained at the associate project manager level all eight years of her employ-
ment, during which time many of her peers with the same or even less experience have been promoted to senior project managers, if not department heads.*

*Back when she was a college undergraduate, Lisa received straight A's
and had an ambition of someday being a manager or supervisor. She began
to work at her current organization right after graduation. Six months later,
she married her childhood sweetheart. Within a year, she had her first child
. . . twelve months later, her second.*

*The years have gone by and her children are now old enough to take the
bus to and from school on their own. She no longer requires the same flexible
schedule. In fact, her husband has started his own business, which means he*

can arrange his schedule to take the kids to and from soccer practice, dance classes, and special events.

Lisa wakes up one day with a realization: she deserves something much better than her current job. She's put in eight solid years and has nothing to show for it. Her boss has never even mentioned potential opportunities for her. She remembers seeing several openings within the company that are at a higher level than her current position. She makes a decision to set up a one-on-one meeting with her boss to discuss how she might apply for those positions and advance in the organization.

Sarah, her manager, happens to be available that morning and welcomes her into her office. She starts off by asking Lisa for a few project updates, which she provides. "Very good—thank you, Lisa. Anything else?" she asks.

"Well, now that you mention it," Lisa says, taking a deep breath. "I've been wondering about my future. I mean . . . what I need to do in order to receive a promotion."

Sarah grins from ear to ear, chuckling under her breath. "A promotion? Why would you want that? You're doing just fine! Everyone thinks you are fine right where you are."

"Um," Lisa considers. "There's the money, for one thing. Also, I think I can do more for the company. I've been here for eight years in the same position."

"There's a reason for that," Sarah replies. "You are fine in your current role and the company relies on you for what you do. Also, you've never shown any interest in advancement."

Lisa begins to feel frustrated. Why is her boss not taking her seriously? "But . . . after all of my time here, I feel I deserve an opportunity to move up. I just saw several manager roles posted that I know I could do well—if I were given the chance."

"Why would you want to do that, Lisa? It's so much pressure. You don't need the headaches. You'll just burn out from the extra hours. You'd have to go through hours of management training. You want to have some energy left for your husband and kids, don't you?"

"My kids are older and Mike, my husband, is now working from home with his new business and is able to help out more," Lisa says. "But that's beside the point. I'm saying I want to do it."

Sarah sits back in her chair. She sips some coffee and then folds her hands in the "steeple position" with fingertips touching to form a triangle. "Listen,

Lisa, I think you are doing fine at what you do . . . but, frankly, I just don't see you as manager material. No one here does. That's not a bad thing. The standards are really high for managers. You don't want to fail and then be out of a job, do you?"

Lisa feels like she has been tossed out her boss's twenty-story window. She can't believe this is how her boss—whom she has trusted—really sees her. She thinks about the worst-case scenario of being terminated if she were to fail as a manager and realizes her family can't afford to be without her income. "I guess you're right," she concedes.

Sarah's smile is restored as she draws the discussion to a close: "Excellent—keep up the fine work, Lisa!"

As Lisa exits her boss's office, she can't help but feel paralyzed and stuck. But what can she do when her boss has such a limited, preconceived notion of who she is and what she can accomplish?

Reinvention is often thought of derogatively or as something to be ashamed of; it implies that a failure has occurred that required correction. In Lisa's case, has she failed at anything? Absolutely not. A combination of things occurred over the years: she chose not to act on her ambitions; she focused on her family life more than her work life; and she lacked the self-esteem to throw herself out there and demonstrate her full capabilities. All of this can be remedied by applying the art of *reinvention*—which does involve a great deal of self-examination and hard work.

There is no stigma attached to reinvention. I submit that we are in a constant state of renewal. Who we are and what we desire for ourselves now could not possibly be the same exact things we sought ten years ago. Tastes change. Circumstances and life stages change. Ambitions change. Curiosities and interests change. Friends come and go. Loved ones are lost and introduced into the world through births and relationships. Why, it would be a shock if we didn't react to so many things happening in the world each and every day.

It takes immense courage to reinvent yourself. You must overcome a significant amount of fear imagining what other people might think of the new person you have become. My response to this: *who the heck cares what they think?*

Clarissa's Corner

Believe me: I worry a great deal of the time and fear many things. I can be a champion pessimist at certain moments, too. I am only human, after all!

Here's my secret: As part of my continuous reinvention, I never allow such emotions to dictate my thoughts or actions. I also never allow other people's comments to cause me worry or fear.

Look at worry and fear this way:

Worry is simply *praying for the things you don't want.*

Fear is *false evidence appearing real.*

Stay fierce and courageous and remember why your goals will be life changing.

It might comfort you to know that the most successful people in the world are all about being fearless when it comes to reinvention, risk taking, and rule breaking on a grand scale. In the 1960s, the Beatles shifted gears and revolutionized music and culture with each and every single and album release while evolving their look to reflect their creative endeavors. Artists such as Cher, David Bowie, Tina Turner, Prince, Madonna, and, currently, Lady Gaga, never settled for just one musical sound or look. They were constantly changing, growing, exploring, testing boundaries, and stretching their creative limits, leaving many risk-averse performers in the dust as one-hit wonders. If they can do it, so can you!

Reinventing Yourself to Become the Authentic You

Of course, as you undergo the reinvention process, you must *remain true to the person you are meant to be.* The goal is not to emulate a star or anyone else, although it is possible to be inspired by someone you admire during your reinvention and to incorporate aspects of them that you like and work for you. If you think pink hair is the *real you,* by all means, go for it and experiment—and don't let anyone burst your bubble!

I have reinvented myself quite a few times in my lifetime, and I couldn't be happier. I've given myself permission to become many different Clarissas. Each time, I faced major challenges—as well as ups and downs—but the efforts were also rewarding from a learning and personal development standpoint. I've been a babysitter, waitress, temp, model, actress, celebrity, talk show host, singer, director, author, speaker, multimedia producer, publisher—and the beat goes on! How many times have I heard people corner me with the following advice: "Just pick one and stick with it, already! You shouldn't be doing so many things. You'll confuse people."

I firmly believe in a person's right to assert and challenge herself. I may not have been an expert or "the best" at any one thing, but I was confident that I could do a whole bunch of things pretty darn well—and I don't regret a single endeavor I attempted.

I'm not for a split-second suggesting that you should try as many things as I have over the years. Going overboard and chasing after the next squirrel—that is, personal or career dreams—like an anxious puppy is definitely not the solution. Every attempt at reinvention must be a means to an end to help you further your vision, purpose, and mission. In other words, the reinvention should already appear on your vision board.

Proactive People Get Ahead

As I indicated earlier in this chapter, Lisa did not make any specific mistakes. She did what she felt was right for herself and family at various stages in her life. In some respects, it could be said that she felt she was forced to settle for the status quo—a sacrifice made by many multi-tasking working moms. Unfortunately, certain impressions form about employees over time, whether they are aware of them or not. Managers, supervisors, department heads, executives, colleagues, and even clients and customers form conclusions based on the following:

- Does she seem ambitious?
- Does she regularly express serious interest in advancement?
- Does she seem passionate and excited about her job?
- Does she put in 110 percent effort all the time?
- Does she speak up at meetings?

- Does she volunteer for "stretch" assignments (projects outside her job description and a bit more advanced)?
- Does she attempt to be visible in the organization?
- Does she seem self-confident in her work interactions?
- Does she make sure her accomplishments and talents are recognized?

In Lisa's case, the answer to all of the above questions is an obvious "no." If she had truly wanted to advance in the company during her eight years, she would have demonstrated more initiative, made her intent clear, proven her mettle, and, perhaps most importantly, tooted her horn. Being steady and reliable and getting the job done may keep the paychecks coming, but it won't get you to the next level. The employees who get ahead in any company are the aggressive ones with fire in the belly who are proactive about providing extra value at all times. They also boast about their accomplishments to anyone who will listen.

Sarah, Lisa's supervisor, seems somewhat baffled that Lisa is asking for a promotion and feels that Lisa has already settled into her passive, lifetime role in the company. One might credibly argue that she is holding her employee back, but the reality is also that *Lisa is holding herself back*, although she believes she is asserting herself during the meeting with her boss. The phrase, "I've been here for many years and do my job really well" says it all to Sarah. Quite simply, it's not going to do anything to sell her case and convince her boss. The same durable wallpaper and carpeting may have adorned the office building and been *fine* for many years, but it doesn't mean they stand out as anything special.

Clearly, Lisa needs to reinvent herself and change her messaging to the world. I don't mean change who she is or pretend to be someone she's not, but rather, Lisa must bring to the surface more of what is already inside of her and allow Sarah—as well as everyone else—to recognize her abilities. In order to change perceptions, she must look at herself from a distance and make a conscious effort to become the person she wishes to be.

How do you reinvent your persona at work or anywhere else? It all starts with one cliché. . . .

Fake It . . .

No doubt you've heard the cliché "Fake it until you make it." Like most overused expressions, there is truth behind it. I believe that all intelligent new hires in a company—especially those fresh out of college—must pretend to be capable and knowledgeable while also admitting that they need to learn a lot about the job and how the company works, as well as receive proper training. "Faking it until you make it" under these circumstances doesn't suggest that you are doing anything wrong or unethical, it simply means that you are making an effort to show that you are worthy enough to belong in the company and are confident in your abilities to accept responsibility.

Reinvention requires a similar type of thinking. If you wish to alter the perceptions others have of you—whether at work or in your personal life—you must *walk the walk* and *talk the talk* as the first step. How you dress and comport yourself means everything. If you don't look and act like manager material, for example, no one will think of you this way.

Lisa, for example, had been going to work every day in faded jeans and a sweatshirt while haphazardly putting her hair in a ponytail and rarely applying makeup. She walked around the office hallways with her shoulders slumped and her eyes turned away from colleagues as they passed by.

Although her company did not have a formal dress code, female and male managers alike all showed up to work in smart casual business attire. Sarah, in particular, was especially conscious of her presentation, wearing snazzy Donna Karan business outfits and grooming her hair and applying makeup as if she had just stepped out of a Beverly Hills beauty salon. She held herself with her chin up and shoulders out, clear indications that she belonged in her role. As noted, she even trained herself to steeple her hands when asserting authority with those who reported to her. In other words, Sarah looked and acted her role and embraced it with pride. She displayed this confident look and swagger from her first day at the company, even when she didn't yet have a clue what she was doing. She succeeded in those early days because she faked it until she made it.

The film *Working Girl*, which starred Melanie Griffith as an ambitious office assistant, may be somewhat dated by today's standards, but the themes behind the story remain as true as ever. When her character, Tess McGill, realizes that Katharine, her boss (portrayed by Sigourney Weaver), has been stealing her ideas, Tess decides to pretend to be her when she breaks her leg while out of town on a ski trip. Since Tess has access to Katharine's apartment and wardrobe, she is able to play the role of hotshot by copying as much as possible of her boss's dress and manner. She even takes to *smelling* like her, dabbing on Katharine's expensive perfume. The ruse is convincing for some time, especially as she makes an important business contact with Jack Trainer (played by Harrison Ford).

Do I suggest going as far as stealing someone else's identity like Tess? No, of course not! However, by studying and learning from others, you can "fake it" just enough to look and act the part until you prove yourself and win the job for real. Often, simple changes in wardrobe, posture, speaking style, facial expression, and manner can build enough confidence to enable you to feel as if you belong in a management-level role. When your boss and colleagues witness the reinvention, they will begin to see you in a renewed light. This is when you must hunker down and become a star performer at your job in order to shine and take the necessary steps to earn that promotion. A supportive boss (unlike what we've seen thus far of Sarah) will mentor an employee like Lisa and provide her with an action plan identifying what it would take for her to get to the next level.

Retrain Your Brain to Reinvent Yourself

Although changing how you look and present yourself is beneficial, it's obviously not enough to complete a full reinvention. Lisa, for example, needs to retrain her brain in order to stop the loop of the negative thought from resurfacing and spinning around in her head.

Dr. Jeffrey Fannin, a neuroscientist and brain performance expert based in the Phoenix, Arizona, area, has some fascinating theories on how retraining your brain can lead to reinvention and ultimate success. Dr. Fannin asserts that any thought that is repeated over and over again becomes a tightly held *belief*, whether one is aware of it or not.

Negative beliefs—especially those based on actual experiences—often become associated with raw emotions. These beliefs, coupled with the emotions, become digitized in the brain as something like a "final recording." Each time something occurs that triggers a resurgence of that thought, the recording plays in your head, accompanied by the same painful emotions. The more frequently the recording plays, the harder it becomes to drown it out and/or delete it because it's such an emotional experience.

According to Dr. Fannin's research, 95 percent of what we say, think, and feel is negative—95 percent! No wonder so many of us have low self-esteem with all of these "recordings" and their associated emotions continuously playing in our heads. As if that's not enough, each thought/emotion carries a seventeen-second vibration that is sent throughout our bodies. Any kind of self-doubt or feeling of disappointment, therefore, creates a ripple effect throughout the body, which may result in stress, anxiety, depression, and, of course, low self-esteem.

See Your Glass as Half Full

We all know a "woe is me" type of negative person who feels the world is conspiring to make her miserable. The poster child for this persona is the character Charlie Brown from Charles M. Shultz's Peanuts comics, who famously said, "I think I'm afraid of being happy because whenever I get too happy something bad always happens."

Dominating Your Daily Demons

You'll need to open up your journal for this exercise. Trust me: it's a powerful one! We want your reinvention to be swift and effective.

Take whatever time you need to write down the following questions in your journal and then thoughtfully answer them. No need to rush.

Once I have completed my transformation . . .

. . . what do I see myself looking like?

. . . what am I wearing?

. . . what facial expression do I have?

. . . what thoughts do I have?

. . . how do I feel about myself?

Once you complete your answers and are satisfied with them, transfer them to a clean sheet of paper. Every time you feel dissatisfied with where you are in life, repeat these statements aloud to yourself three times. Your reinvention process will begin the first time you do this, as you already have a picture in your mind of what the "new you" looks and feels like, so you will work even harder to achieve it without allowing any demons to stand in your way.

Science dictates that when you think bad things will happen, they usually do. In an earlier chapter, I referenced the law of attraction; well, the opposite also holds true. If negative thoughts and emotions are constantly replaying in your mind, you are attracting all of that bad mojo. Dr. Fannin believes that if the phrase "Nothing good ever happens to me" is drummed in your head, it becomes a self-fulfilling prophecy and nothing good will ever happen to you.

Let's revisit Lisa's story. Do you think she remembers how Sarah ended their meeting with the obligatory "Keep up the fine work!"—or, instead, the sting of her boss's earlier statement "frankly, I just don't see you as manager material. No one here does"?

Unquestionably, Lisa went back to her desk after the meeting feeling deflated and like a total failure. In her mind, the effort resulted in slamming headlong into a brick wall. She probably will replay Sarah telling her she is not management material in her head during her commute home, as she recounts the story to her husband during dinner, when she goes to sleep at night, and when she wakes up in the morning. In fact, each time she communicates with her boss—through email, phone, or in person—those words and the emotion of feeling like a failure probably echo in her head with increasing volume and power. The repetition is so convincing that her boss's statement becomes absolute fact to Lisa's subconscious, even though it is not.

When he was a child, acclaimed motivational speaker and bestselling author Les Brown was diagnosed as being "mentally disabled" and referred to as "DT," meaning "dumb twin." *Les Brown*, of all people!

Les had the fortune of encountering one teacher who stopped the "DT" recording in his head by telling him not to listen to anyone or to allow other people's stories to affect and influence him. It's a good

Clar-ion Call

Remember that *fail* stands for *first attempt in learning*. No one gets anything 100 percent perfect on the first try. Reinvention takes time and practice. You may have to try more than once to succeed. Stay determined. Never give up!

thing that teacher showed up when she did or else Les Brown might not have grown up to become such a major inspiration to so many people.

Myth Busters

Dr. Fannin offers seven myths to help you retrain your brain and counter painful, recurring thoughts that hold you back. I encourage you to copy these seven myths and place them in your journal or on your desk as frequent reminders.

1. *Myth #1: Intelligence is fixed.* We learn and improve ourselves every single day that we live and breathe. We are constantly growing, which means that we are only getting smarter from our studies and experiences.
2. *Myth #2: We use only 10 percent of our brains.* There is *zero* scientific evidence proving that we use only a small percentage of our brains. This is a fallacy. In fact, science to date indicates the opposite is probably true—we use about 90 percent of our brains.
3. *Myth #3: Mistakes are failures.* This one is a doozy! If everyone considered him- or herself a failure after each mistake, nothing would ever be accomplished. Thomas Edison famously failed 999 times before successfully inventing the incandescent light bulb.
4. *Myth #4: Knowledge is power.* This is a manipulation used by people with authority who wish to control and assert their power over others. If you have less knowledge about a subject, it doesn't mean you are weak; it indicates only that you have more to learn.
5. *Myth #5: Learning new things is difficult (or the cliché: "Old dogs can't learn new tricks").* Bo Gilbert, a woman in Birmingham, the United Kingdom, modeled professionally for the first time in her life for England's *Vogue* magazine when she was *one hundred years*

old. In my opinion, Bo is a true supermodel! If a centenarian can learn how to pose for a major magazine, surely you can believe you are capable of doing anything to which you set your mind.

6. *Myth #6: Criticism matters*. Sarah probably believed she was helping Lisa by providing "constructive criticism." Not only was her statement unsupportive, insulting, and unbecoming of a true leader, it was completely irrelevant. Her boss is not the be-all and end-all. Lisa can delete that comment from her mind and immediately begin her reinvention. She should not for a second be deterred in her quest for a promotion. If Sarah continues to keep Lisa down even after she has performed a litany of exceptional accomplishments, it will be the company's loss when she takes her talents elsewhere and it struggles to replace her.

7. *Myth #7: Genius is born*. Utter nonsense. IQ tests are not any kind of measure of genius at writing, painting, composing, acting, dancing, innovating, street smarts, and thousands of other areas. All babies are born with the *potential* for genius at *something*. The question is how an individual's genius might be brought out and fostered to its fullest potential.

What Does Reinvention Look Like?

Your reinvention can look like anything you wish it to be: your hair, your face, your clothing, your accessories, how you walk, how you talk, and so much more. Small changes can make a big difference.

You may be fortunate enough to have a close friend who works in a beauty parlor as a hairdresser or markup artist. It's possible your present hair salon may be well-equipped to help you with what you need, but it also may be awkward for you to ask your regular professionals to rethink everything they have been doing for you for years. Although they may have the skill and be receptive to creative thinking, they may have some residual preconceived notions that hold them back from thinking outside the box. Personally, I think that if you are going all out to reinvent yourself, you probably would be best served by starting with a clean slate: someone who is highly recommended and who truly wants to impress you.

So, where do you begin? You could let the makeover professionals "wing it," but that might entail greater risk than what you have in mind. Going in with some kind of advance directional plan is always a good idea.

You could look through the typical hairstyling and treatment books or simply search online for looks that seem to best fit the messages you wish to convey. Another possibility is using Photoshop on photos of yourself to test out how you look with a new hair color or hairstyle. The good news is that you can play around with different looks until you land on what you like.

Next, I recommend you let it sit for a couple of days and come back to it with a fresh eye. If the image still seems like something exciting to you after that, go for it! If you have any doubt, don't do it—at least until you are comfortable. The worst thing to do is to try to reinvent yourself and not feel confident before heading in. Even if you look spectacular afterward, you may not be able to pull it off because you aren't carrying your new look with pride.

A Final Note on Reinvention

As I stated earlier in this chapter, reinvention should not be looked upon as a one-time thing. We are constantly learning, developing, and reacting to the world around us, along with our circumstances in life. The best times to reinvent are when we are attempting to give ourselves a brand-new start, as in the following types of scenarios:

- When heading back into the workforce after time off or time away.
- When making a career change.
- When seeking a promotion or otherwise looking to get ahead.
- When leaving a job (such as after being laid off).
- When undergoing a major life change, including a breakup or divorce, the passing of a loved one, a move to a new city, or recovery from an illness.
- When feeling stagnant or at a dead end in a current job or career.
- When feeling bored and listless.

In other words, you can happily reinvent yourself at any time and at any age—and you can do it multiple times throughout your life. My only caution is not to do it *too* often—such as every year—as that would be confusing to you and everyone in your sphere. Nor do I suggest flitting back and forth among past reinventions; you should always be thinking in terms of moving yourself forward. Your goal is always to gain more clarity about the person you were meant to be, not to attempt to take on multiple personas. Once you reach superstar level of fame and recognition like Madonna and Lady Gaga, then all bets are off, and you can reinvent all you like!

Affirmation: I Will Become My Best Self

I will become the person I was always meant to be.
I will not settle for less than I deserve.
I know that I deserve only the best for myself.
I am not what others think of me.
I was created for greatness and to inspire others.
I am excited about who I am becoming as I map out my future.
It's okay to say "yes" to getting up, moving on, and never looking back.
I will do what is necessary to complete my reinvention and conquer the world.

REview

- Be fearless when you begin to reinvent yourself.
- Recognize that there isn't any stigma to reinvention.
- Fake it until you make it in order to jump-start becoming the person you were meant to be.
- Consider a physical makeover—even a small change—when reinventing yourself in order to alter other people's impressions of you.
- Counter negative thoughts before they connect with negative emotions and become beliefs.
- Copy the seven myths as a reminder to yourself whenever you feel stuck or down.

~

CHAPTER SEVEN

REinforce

Rich people have small TVs and big libraries, and poor people have small libraries and big TVs.

—Zig Ziglar, author and motivational speaker

Selena is a single working mom of two young children. Somehow, she manages two minimum-wage jobs: one full time and the other part time on weekends. In spite of putting in so many work hours each week without a single day off, she and her family scrape by with barely enough to pay the mortgage and other monthly bills. On top of that, her kids have medical issues that require expensive doctor visits and medications that aren't fully covered by insurance. When a major appliance inevitably breaks down—washer, dryer, dishwasher, and so on—she puts the expense on one of her three credit cards. When the toilet backs up or her roof leaks, once again she pulls a plastic card out of her purse to pay the repair person.

Selena is a caring mom who feels guilty about not spending enough quality time with her kids due to her work schedule. On Saturday evenings, she treats the kids to a big dinner out, followed by a movie. At the theater, she inevitably caters to her kids' requests for the big tub of popcorn and extra-large sodas—not to mention overpriced bags and boxes of candy. On Sunday evenings, she's too exhausted to prepare food, so once again she takes the kids out to dinner, followed by a visit to the local ice cream shop where they enjoy a five-scoop sundae.

Birthdays and Christmases are extra celebrations in Selena's household because she goes all out on gifts for her two kids. She purchases the most expensive videogames and toys—at full retail price because she doesn't have time to price shop and look for bargains—as well as $100 sneakers and designer clothing. She wants the best for her children and does not want them to look or feel like they are lacking in anything.

At the end of the year, Selena sees that she hardly has a dime in her savings account. Meanwhile, she's nearly maxed out all three of her credit cards.

No matter how hard she tries and how many hours a week she works, Selena cannot seem to dig herself out of her financial hole. She's borrowed all she can from friends and family and can't afford to take out another loan or line of credit. She feels burned out, stressed out, and poor. She frets that it's only a matter of time before she and her kids end up on the street, homeless, and waiting in food bank lines. Though she manages to keep a positive front to her coworkers and family, deep down she feels ashamed of herself and like an utter failure.

What can Selena do to improve her life situation and reinforce her devastated self-esteem?

I don't pretend to be a financial manager, accountant, or any other kind of authority on money matters. But one thing I do understand well is the relationship between self-esteem and financial stability. On one hand, being wealthy doesn't automatically make a person happy and content. On the other, we all need enough money to pay our bills, support our families, and, yes, nourish ourselves and feel like accomplished, successful people.

My heart goes out to Selena and everyone like her around the world. They work themselves so hard yet have nothing left in the tank for themselves—emotionally, physically, and financially. What does all of this labor get them, except to eke by another month?

From my experience with Selena, she is a strong, highly capable woman who is doing everything she feels she can to keep her family above water and content. At the same time, her lack of savings and the stress caused by surging debt are taking a severe toll on her mental and emotional state, which, over time, will wreak havoc on her physical health.

From what I know of Selena, she was born with ample self-esteem and grew up in a stable, supportive middle-class household that fostered her sense of self. Unfortunately, her confidence ebbs more and more with every overdue bill notice she receives and every declined credit card purchase. In her case, the *reinforce* step of the regime is absolutely critical. If she doesn't take immediate action to improve her financial status and reinforce her submerged positive mind-set, I fear she and her family will be on the brink of ruin.

The Scarcity Mind-Set

A 2015 study by Oxford University and the Joseph Rowntree Foundation revealed that there is a direct correlation between poverty and what their researchers refer to as "the scarcity mind-set." Several things occur that add significant momentum to the downward spiral. The first is the intense focus on short-term survival, which results in a shortened attention span and a decline in decision-making ability. Stress leads to an emphasis on short-term planning rather than consideration of the long-term future.

Once a person is spiraling downward as a result of "the scarcity mind-set," the short-term thinking leads to career stagnation, if not failure. She begins to "negative self-stereotype," which essentially means walking around with a dark cloud over her head. Her lack of confidence worsens even more as a result of her perception that a stigma is associated with being poor.

Selena, in particular, blames herself for her state of affairs and is convinced that her fate is a life of scarcity. She has boxed herself in so deeply that she can't see out the top to envision any kind of plan for a brighter future. But there is hope for Selena and her family. In order for her to crawl her way out of the box, she must first clear her mind with powerful reinforcement tools that once again have her feeling confident, capable, and in control of her future.

Money Is an Illusion

Too often we think of money as something tangible that appeals to the five senses:

- *Touch*: We can hold paper money in our hands.
- *Smell*: We love the smell of green bills (no matter how dirty they may actually be!).
- *Taste*: No, we don't literally eat and digest money, but we do think of it in terms of using it to buy food. There is also the phrase "I can practically taste it" uttered in the context of anticipating a large intake of cash.
- *Hearing*: Obviously, money is an inanimate object and doesn't make any sounds on its own, but the idea of money conjures the alluring sound of fanning bills in one's hand.
- *Sight*: Everyone has a visual of what stacks of money look like; many people dream of having access to such piles of cash.

One powerful tool to counter the psychological and sensory impact of money is to separate the *idea* of it in terms of the senses and emotions apart from wants, desires, and needs. If money were considered a cold and distant concept—an illusion, perhaps—it would have less control over a person and, therefore, reduced impact.

"*What?!*" you are likely protesting. "Clarissa—earlier in the regime you told me to have a vision, purpose, and mission. Can't making lots of money be a big part of a person's main goal?"

My answer: *no*. Certainly, you require some money as you work toward fulfilling your vision, purpose, and mission, and visualizing what being prosperous looks like is a fine concept. Whether you are willing to admit it or not, however, this is not the true end result of your vision. Your real vision is something in the arena of living your specific passionate career dream, finding the love of your life, and so forth. Money is a means to the end, not the other way around.

By separating your senses and emotions from money, your financial situation will have much less control over you and your psyche. Even better, if your financial situation happens to be dire, carving the senses and emotions out of the equation lifts all of the blame and weight of it off your shoulders. In the end, with a freer mind, you will make better, smarter, faster, and more level-headed financial decisions.

As billionaire investor Warren Buffett once said, "If you cannot control your emotions, you cannot control your money." This statement is just as true for a supermarket cashier and gas station attendant as it is for a wealthy Wall Street tycoon.

Dominating Your Daily Demons

Sometimes the temptation to spend is just too great—even if you have tremendous willpower regarding other areas of your life. Now it's easier than ever to buy luxuries based on impulse. With online purchasing, you don't even need to leave your home! It only takes a few seconds to drag an item into a virtual shopping cart and then click the buy button to make a purchase. It's like living inside a chocolate factory when you're on a diet.

How do you curb such impulse spending to help control your money? The most effective albeit extreme method is to cancel your credit cards on those sites or even block the websites entirely.

For most people, however, it's not realistic to completely block a site such as amazon.com, where necessities often overlap with luxuries. I get it!

An easier way to approach this is to create a simple rule: *leave any purchase in your shopping cart for a minimum of forty-eight hours.* In all likelihood, you will forget about clicking the "buy" button during the two-day time frame, which means the next time you see it in the shopping cart, you'll crave it much less and change your mind. You may even ask yourself, "What on earth was I thinking?!"

Start Planning Today

Now that money has lost its power over you, it is time to begin reinforcing how to make it work *for* you. It all starts with common sense, basic knowledge, and, yes, planning. I don't expect you to become as financially well-versed as a CPA, CFO, or financial planner or even to take a training course in Excel (though it's not a bad idea and probably would be beneficial for you). Instead, I propose that you become comfortable with money and financially literate as it applies to having a basic understanding of cash in (revenue, such as salary) and cash out (spending, such as monthly bills).

You may recall Nora from chapter 5, who embodies the *reaffirm* stage of the regime. She looks to her coach for practical guidance and career advice. Although this is an excellent way to help you unlock your potential and set you on your path, not everyone has access to such resources to gain positive reinforcement. Hiring a coach is the last thing on the minds of people struggling to pay bills each month.

Selena, our heroine from earlier in this chapter, is obviously not in any kind of financial position to be able to afford a coach. But she does need help. On the plus side, she cares a great deal about her financial situation and is diligent about paying her bills to the best of her ability. Unfortunately, sensory and emotional overloads and bill paying aside, that's the extent of her financial connection. She hasn't done anything to demonstrate that *she is the boss of her money.* She isn't paying nearly enough attention to the nuances of where her money is going nor is she looking at her cash in/cash out dynamic from a strategic point of view.

The first stage of any budget plan is to write down your monthly earnings, expenses, and purchases and divide them into three columns. Selena jotted the first two columns down without any difficulty. She was in for a rude awakening when she hit column three: the list kept going on and on and on—and she wasn't even sure she was remembering everything. Many of the amounts seemed insignificant at the time, but they sure did pile up when added together. Here is just a sampling of the first few items in column three:

Eight dinners with kids: $52 (average for each) × 4 weeks = $208
Movie with kids: $26 × 4 weeks = $104
Popcorn, candy, and drinks at the movie theater: $31 × 4 weeks = $124
Daily morning Starbucks coffee: $35 per week × 4 weeks = $140
Gifts/clothing/accessories for kids: $200
Total: $776

Selena was spending $776 each month in just those five areas! Selena nearly passed out when she saw that number—and it doesn't even include all of the other purchases made throughout the month. Suffice it to say, she didn't earn anything close to the amount needed from her two jobs to sustain such exorbitant spending. "No wonder I'm so broke and in debt!" she exclaimed.

After recovering from the initial shock, she came to an amazing realization: "Look at all of the money I'll have back in my pocket if I choose not to spend on these things every month. I'll be able to pay off the debt—and even put in for some savings. I'll finally have *control* over my money."

Once this light switch clicked on for Selena, she began to feel her old self returning. She started to feel confident and empowered. She now saw that all of her hard work, accompanied by financial literacy, could ultimately reinforce her self-esteem.

Clarissa's Corner

Do you know how much you have in your savings and checking accounts at all times? Do you know what your monthly earnings are versus your total spending on bills? Do you know how much you owe in credit card debt and the interest you are paying?

Knowledge about Your Money = Control and Empowerment

The money you have left over each month after you've paid your expenses (including food and medications) is your *free cash*. Spending any more than that amount only adds to your debt. This means that all other purchases—especially entertainment—are *luxuries*. The more you spend on luxuries, the less you will have for needs and wants. As for the savings account and retirement plan—well, you won't ever have those if you don't pay enough attention to your finances.

You can have the occasional well-deserved luxury, but only after you've tightened your belt to get rid of debt and gradually added to your savings and retirement accounts.

Practical Matters

Of course, Selena and her family would have to work together to cut back on the excessive spending on meals, movies, snacks, and other extras. That's not to say she would have to eliminate *everything*. That could be equally detrimental to her family's mental state. Everyone needs a break and a reasonable reward every now and then.

Practically speaking, Selena knew right off the bat that she couldn't blame her kids for all of the money leaks: $200 a month for her daily Starbucks coffee amounted to $2,400 over the course of a year. She could easily sacrifice that by settling for the free coffee offered in her office breakroom. Was it as satisfying to her as the Starbucks cup? Not at all—but it would be well worth dropping this particular expenditure in favor of the big picture. With that kind of savings after a full year, she could afford a much-needed summer vacation with her kids!

Cutting the frequent dinners and movies proved to be a sore spot with her kids. They loved going to their favorite restaurants and seeing at least four new film releases a month. Selena was able to compromise, however, and reduce the number of dinners to five per month and the movies to two. Instead of spending $124 every month on goodies at the theater's snack counter, they chopped the amount down to $17.50. Once again, the savings over the stretch of a full year were dramatic.

Selena promised to squirrel away all of the extra unspent money into four new columns: credit card payments; her savings account; investments in her kids' college funds; and the long-awaited family vacation. She consolidated her credit card debt into one account, ditched two of her credit cards, and swore off using the remaining card except for emergencies.

All of this may seem like pretty basic stuff, but I've found that many people aren't disciplined enough to create realistic budgets for themselves and their families. They aren't taking the simple step of keeping track of their purchases. They also tend to dole out extra "found" money (i.e., bonuses) as soon as they get them because the lump of bills burns holes in their purses and wallets.

Here is a simple compromise. Instead of blowing all of that found money in one shot, you could choose to splurge just $5 on that Starbucks latte—a one-time treat—without feeling a smidgeon of guilt. At this point, you should feel good about stepping up to the barista counter to order and receive your cherished beverage. You've *earned* it, after all—and the expense skims only a small amount off the top (forgive the pun!) of whatever money you've received.

Always Place High Value on Yourself

The worst thing a person can do is belittle her value by undercharging for her work time or for her entrepreneurial products or services. If you fall into this category, you are not doing anyone—especially yourself—any favors. Yes, you are leaving money on the table—but that isn't the main issue.

Earlier in this chapter, I emphasized the point that money should never be regarded as an object that should be conflated with human senses or emotion. However, that doesn't mean money lacks the power to generate what I shall refer to as *invisible energy*. How you value yourself internally and externally to the world becomes an energy stream that either jolts you with a positive charge or floods you with negative particles. This impacts how you comport yourself, as well as how you are perceived by others.

Consider this: think back to a time in your life when you were praised by a supervisor and rewarded with a promotion, raise, and/or bonus. How did your mind and body feel? How did you hold yourself in the hallway afterward? Did you burst at the seams with excitement for when you could share the good news with your significant other, a close friend, a sibling, or a parent?

Without a doubt, the reinforcement of a supervisor at work can carry a person's spirits for several days, if not weeks. You feel like you are on top of the world. You might upgrade your work wardrobe and burst through the front door at work early with a giddy smile and extra skip in your step. Your supervisor will then take notice of your positive energy and feel like the accolades and financial reward were a wise investment in your future and for the organization. You have reinforced your supervisor's confidence in you, which will pay everyone back in dividends over time.

Clar-ion Call

On a blank page in your journal or on a clean sheet of paper, write down the following questions:

- What must I learn in order to increase my financial value to others?
- What skills must I upgrade to earn more money?
- What beliefs and habits must I reinforce to show people that I am worth more than I am currently receiving?
- What beliefs and habits must I release that are holding me back from earning more money?

- Whom do I know who can become cheerleaders and help support me to achieve my financial goals?

Next, write down your answers to each question. In doing so, you are reinforcing that you are in control of your ability to earn more money and have various pathways toward achieving your goal. Put a sticky note on this page in your journal to remind yourself of these goals and determine how far you are progressing on a monthly basis.

One note of caution: do not assign a specific time frame to achieving the desired results. It takes time for your efforts to be recognized, and there are timing issues and politics involved in these decisions within every organization. Bide your time and don't rush or force it (i.e., by storming into your supervisor's office and demanding a raise on the spot). Do the best you can at all times and never allow yourself to be discouraged. It will happen, if it's meant to be. If you don't get the increase after a significant period of time—such as a year—it may be wise to start applying for positions at other companies where you will have better opportunity to obtain the reinforcement you need and deserve.

This all leads to my assertion that, unless you are in a challenging financial situation, you should never settle for less money than you are worth. You should never leave money on the table in any negotiation, whether it's regarding your salary or the value of your products or services. You will always get paid in direct proportion to the service and value that you bring to the marketplace.

If you are not earning enough in your current role, it may be because you are not demonstrating enough value for your services, knowledge, and expertise. Or you simply haven't been releasing your energy in such a way that it communicates to people the message: "I bring a ton of value to every task I complete." The more value you place on yourself, the greater others will value you in turn.

Affirmation: I Am Worth It

I will create a budget and stick to it.

I will get never settle for less than what I deserve.

I will do what it takes to achieve my full value.

I will be in control of my finances at all times.

I will not allow my emotions and senses to dictate my relationship with money.

I will never sacrifice my health or well-being to save money.

I will be protective of the money I have rightfully earned.

I will reward my mind, body, and spirit with reasonable gifts I can afford when I need or deserve them.

REview

- Recognize when you are stuck in a "scarcity mind-set."
- Reduce the negative impact of money by not thinking about it in terms of your senses and emotions.
- Begin to reinforce your relationship with money by writing down all of your monthly expenses and creating a realistic budget.
- Cut back on nonessential spending until your finances are on stable ground.
- Reinforce your self-esteem by doing justice to your true value in the workplace.

CHAPTER EIGHT

~

REpeat

Habit is the intersection of knowledge (what to do), skill (how to do), and desire (want to do).

—Stephen R. Covey, author of
7 Habits of Highly Effective People

Kate, a bright woman in her thirties, has always struggled with her self-confidence. One of her main attributes is her level of self-awareness; unfortunately, this mostly concerns recognition of her greatest weakness—lack of organizational skills.

She has purchased every organizing, decluttering, and simplifying-your-life book on the market and has tried every tip offered in blogs, websites, and magazines. Nothing seems to work for her. Her life is a mess of scattered Post-its, planners, notebooks, memo pads, and notes on the refrigerator. She's tried adding reminder alarms on her phone, except she always seems to type the wrong times and days; turn off her alerts when they are needed the most; or misplace her mobile phone entirely.

Although the quality of her work is good, Kate receives poor-to-average annual reviews from her supervisor because she misses deadlines and arrives late and bedraggled to meetings and, sometimes, to the office in the morning. She has a reputation for joining videoconferences late because she can't find the meeting links in her inbox. Even her friends have grown frustrated with her unreliability, dubbing her "late Kate."

Every year, Kate makes a New Year's resolution to become more organized—and each time she fails and becomes angrier with herself. How can she turn things around?

Approximately half of all Americans make New Year's resolutions. Take a wild guess how many of them actually are successful: less than 10 percent. This begs the question: *why bother?*

In my experience, the issue is not the concept of New Year's resolutions themselves. I think it's a wonderful idea to start each year with a fresh slate and new and improved goals. However, if "becoming more organized" has been at the top of your list more than once without sustained improvement, you have been wasting your effort.

For some people, lack of organizational skills is an executive cognitive dysfunction that was never officially diagnosed and treated. For others, it's a matter of prioritization: it's simply easier and less time consuming to let things go and say you'll put them in their proper places later on. Although there is no one magical formula to getting 100 percent organized that works for everyone in all circumstances, there is one step in the regime that can make a significant difference: *repeat*. If you follow the practical guidance in this chapter, you will begin to notice small improvements in your lifestyle that will have a big impact on your level of organizational success and, therefore, your self-esteem.

Rinse and Repeat

It's simply not possible to write down a New Year's resolution, vow to make it work, and then expect it to happen. There are two reasons for this: lack of continuous motivation and the challenge of overcoming the old way of doing something, which usually means breaking a long-standing habit.

Kate, the woman referenced at the beginning of this chapter, is wired to be disorganized. It doesn't matter whether it's due to an unresolved executive functioning issue, lack of prioritization, or both; the simple fact is that she is locked into a repeating pattern, which has become a seemingly irreversible habit. And we all know how difficult it can be to break *any* kind of habit. The only way to accomplish this is by adhering to the following steps:

1. Create a *new routine every day, at the same time* that involves a simple, repeatable process.
2. Establish strong motivators to facilitate and support the new routine.
3. Reward yourself periodically for sticking to the routine.
4. Get right back on the horse if you miss a day.
5. Avoid beating yourself up if you face any setbacks.

These steps mean that you don't have to forego your New Year's resolutions; instead, simply convert them into repeatable actions and activate and enable them to become second nature. Establish monthly resolutions instead of annual ones, if that is helpful. Think about it in terms of a professional athlete or musician. Few people can hit a baseball like a professional major league ballplayer without years of substantial training in a batting cage and using a tee over and over again. No one plays violin in the New York Philharmonic without putting in endless hours of arduous instruction and practice. Every dancer in the Paris Opera Ballet must first endure six months of training and then pass a comprehensive exam prior to admission to the program.

This is a way of saying that any activity worth perfecting takes a great deal of energy and repetition to become habit and ultimately stick. This applies to everything from simple tasks—such as flossing every day and ensuring on-time arrival at work—to mastering a talent, sport, skill, or craft. It all starts with good habits repeated on a daily basis.

Grab More Free Time!

Ben Franklin famously wrote, "It is easier to prevent bad habits than it is to break them." I would go a step further and assert, "It is more *painful* to break bad habits than it is to prevent them."

While I'm referencing Franklin, I should mention that he and I share an important habit: waking up at 5:00 a.m. every morning. This is not an easy thing to do! I relish my sleep as much as the next person, and yet I've come to realize the benefits of how much more I get done by waking up so early. Not only do I give myself a head start on my day, I become so much more productive because I have fewer distractions at that time when everyone in my time zone is still in dreamland.

Don't worry. I'm not asking you to wake up at 5:00 a.m. like I do. But what would happen if you were to set your alarm for just *one hour earlier* each day—and actually force yourself out of bed? You'd "find" an extra hour in your day—and you can do anything you want with it, including writing in your journal, working on your vision board, getting a head start on your morning routine, or anything else you like. After just one week, you'll have added seven hours of productive time to your list of weekly accomplishments, which adds up to twenty-eight a month and 336 during the course of a year. Imagine what you could accomplish with that extra 336 hours—you could do yoga, start jogging, or even complete the novel you started ten years ago.

If you are someone like Kate, an extra hour means a lot more time to prepare for the day and arrive at work. The incentives for doing this are both tangible and intangible, as well as short- and long-term. Kate will feel a sense of accomplishment by regularly arriving at the office on time and, eventually, her supervisor will start to take notice that she is turning things around.

Feelings of accomplishment alone may not provide enough motivation out of the starting gate, which means setting in place bonus rewards at various benchmark dates that won't blow your budget. For example, your calendar might look something like this:

- One week: a tall mocha at Starbucks
- One month: the new pair of shoes you've had your eye on
- Six months: dinner and drinks at your favorite restaurant
- One year: a spa weekend

If you happen to be a night owl and do your best work in the evening, that's perfectly fine. Do what is right for you to work at your optimal level while ensuring you are still getting a good night's sleep. (Most medical practitioners recommend seven hours for an adult, seven to eight hours for sixty-five and older, and up to nine for a child.) What I'm suggesting is that you give yourself an extra hour each day and be mindful of how you spend that gift. So, if you are accustomed to waking up at eight, turn the alarm back to seven. If you are one of the millions of people who hits the snooze button for five more minutes of sleep that end up becoming another lost hour, you must retrain your brain to make that forbidden. It may sound painful to ditch the snooze button, but, trust me, the time you are frittering away in bed is far worse.

Your time should be regarded as one of the most precious commodities you own and can control. This translates into the necessity of creating a daily and weekly schedule of events on a whiteboard to ensure you arrive on time wherever you are expected to show up; meet deadlines; complete tasks; and set mini-goals toward achieving your vision. As with the routines of major league sluggers, violinists with the New York Philharmonic, and dancers with the Paris Ballet, you are creating a tailor-made schedule for yourself that involves *repetition*, which means you are converting each activity into a positive habit.

In the *Karate Kid* films, sensei Mr. Miyagi famously teaches his young pupil, Daniel, karate by having him "wax on, wax off" his car. On the surface, Daniel seems to be performing mundane manual labor. In reality, however, Mr. Miyagi is teaching the teenager a host of things simultaneously, namely: that things are not always what they seem; martial arts blocking techniques; how to breathe properly and relax during activities; and muscle memory.

Creating a schedule and giving yourself the gift of an extra hour a day may seem pointless, but doing so consistently enables you to accomplish so much more than you ever thought possible, which will make your self-esteem soar. Emblazon this in your memory:

Repetition = Excellence

Dominating Your Daily Demons

If you slip up one day and don't wake up an hour earlier, do not punish yourself! It's only one hour of one day. You still have 364 others each year to show what you are made of. I don't suggest making up for it by waking two hours earlier the following day, as that defeats the purpose of *repetition*. All you need to do is clear your mind and reset the alarm an hour earlier the following morning. You'll thank me later!

Putting Mind, Body, and Spirit on Autopilot

As wise Mr. Miyagi would say, "Lesson not just karate only. Lesson for whole life! Whole life have balance, everything be better."

The repetition part of my regime applies to all aspects of your well-being: mind, body, and spirit. If one aspect is out of alignment, the rest falters along with it. In order to love yourself, you must demonstrate it through self-care. This starts and ends with good habits that we repeat on a daily basis. Let's work on creating a balanced and better you!

Clar-ion Call

To make your bed or not to make your bed—that is the question!

I vote for establishing the routine of making your bed every morning. When you make your bed in the morning, you are signaling the start of the day. Not only does it look better to have a made bed, it feels better, too, as you gain a sense of closure and pride in having completed a task. I know, it's easy—for most people, anyway—but it's an accomplishment that has a positive impact on your psyche, which translates into *order*. If making your bed is part of your morning ritual, it moves you right into the next task in your morning routine.

For the remainder of this chapter, I guide you through repeatable actions that will have a positive impact on mind, body, and soul.

Food

Remember I told you earlier in this book that I wasn't referring to *regimen* in the strict, arduous sense of the word? Well, I will stick to that promise—including suggestions regarding what you eat.

For starters: I won't preach to you about the importance of breakfast. Unless your energy levels are low by 11:00 a.m., you can choose to forego breakfast on one condition: if it's already your comfortable habit to skip it. If, however, you are erratic about eating breakfast—or any meal, for that matter—you may have a problem. As living, breathing animals—and yes, we count in that category—we need regular

feeding times. The more irregular our eating schedules, the more confused our metabolism becomes, and our brains and bodies suffer the
consequences—especially if this state makes us stressed or anxious,
causing us to binge-eat the wrong foods.

What are the wrong foods, you ask? Eating anything in excess is a
bad idea, particularly sugar (i.e., chocolate, cake, cookies), processed
foods (i.e., anything with refined vegetable oils, most bagged snack
foods, hot dogs), and fried foods (i.e., French fries, breaded or battered
foods, chicken wings). Sodas of any kind—regular or diet—should also
be avoided, as they are loaded with chemicals and both regular and
diet versions can contribute to weight gain. If you must have sugary
products, limit the intake to just a couple of grams of dark chocolate
(which is good for the heart and contains antioxidants when consumed
in small amounts).

So, what are the right foods to eat? Aside from the foods mentioned
above, eating everything in moderation is okay (unless you have high
blood pressure or diabetes, in which you should greatly reduce, if not
completely avoid, salt and sugar). Ensure you are receiving enough of
the following: protein from fish, cheese, lean unprocessed meats, or
another type of plant-based protein (56 grams for the average man;
46 for the average woman); fruits and vegetables (1½–2 cups of fruit
per day for nutrients such as vitamin C and potassium and 2–3 cups of
vegetables per day for nutrients such as vitamin B, iron, and calcium);
carbohydrates (no more than 325 grams per day); and fiber (25–30
grams from food).

Most importantly, you must drink enough water (15½ cups for a man;
11½ cups for a woman) to properly hydrate your body, maintain your
weight, feel energetic, and enable your brain to function at its best. A
couple of cups of coffee or tea are fine, but be careful about caffeine, as
it can cause jitteriness and increase stress and anxiety while potentially
altering your sleep patterns. (Personally, I prefer to drink decaf green
tea every day for its antioxidant properties.) I won't lecture you about
the evils of alcohol (which I happen to avoid), except to say that you
need to be safe and smart while drinking and not overdo it (14 drinks
per week for a man; 7 for a woman).

Clarissa's Corner

Certain foods are inherently bad for your body, mind, and soul, even though they may feel like a quick fix. That doesn't mean you have to avoid the foods you love entirely!

When in doubt, make it yourself. I make my own chocolate (less sugar, more antioxidants), yogurt (to avoid unnecessary sugar), kefir (a fermented drink made from milk that has probiotic properties promoting good gut health), and condiments (ketchup, mustard, and mayonnaise to avoid fructose, additives, and fats).

Finally, when in doubt—especially if you have symptoms of a medical condition, lethargy, sleeplessness, pain, weight gain/loss, or unusually high stress—consult with your trusted physician or nutritionist to see if you need to adjust your diet.

What's Up, Doc?

I cannot emphasize enough the importance of annual medical checkups and biannual dental cleanings/examinations. Murphy's law is that the one time you don't head to the doctor's office is when a known or unknown issue starts to fester and become a real problem. A regular physical exam must become habitual: you should have one at roughly the same time each year and avoid canceling it.

One of the regrets many people have is not taking good care of their teeth when they are young and have the chance. Brushing and flossing regularly are not optional. The alternative, tooth decay, can lead to all sorts of dreaded gum and tooth problems that require expensive and often painful procedures. Biannual dental visits are essential because dentists and hygienists have equipment that can remove the plaque and tartar that even the best brushing and flossing can't. One skipped dental visit can mean an unnecessary cavity forms—or something far worse. Your mouth and smile are vital to maintaining healthy self-esteem, so treat your teeth with extra-special care!

Get on Up

We're all busy people! There isn't any excuse for not exercising at the same time every day for thirty minutes—or every other day, at minimum. You can do *something* to keep your blood flowing and prevent your muscles from atrophying.

Most of us spend a significant portion of our day sitting at a desk and looking at a screen: a phone, a laptop, a tablet, and so on. Being sedentary for prolonged periods of time can lead to weight gain and tension in the neck and back, which explains why so many people head to chiropractic offices each year. Meanwhile, the simple act of standing up and walking every now and then can help burn calories and increase blood flow. Most medical authorities agree that even just thirty minutes of movement a day can elevate your mood and provide as much of an energy boost as a two-ounce piece of dark chocolate.

Sometimes your job requires you to sit for prolonged periods of time—whether a supervisor is hovering over you or you just need to meet a deadline. I understand completely; we've all been there. If you simply cannot stand up every fifteen minutes for a quick stretch or walk around the office, look into whether your company can provide an ergometric chair to provide proper support. Better yet, if your company—or you, if you happen to own your own business—has the budget for it, an adjustable desk that rises with the use of a simple lever enables you to alternate standing and sitting while working.

Being sedentary is an *acquired habit*. The human body has evolved over hundreds of thousands of years to hunt and gather—not to hunch in a chair typing on a laptop. This makes it even more vital for you to incorporate standing, stretching, meditation, and walking breaks throughout your daily schedule. If you take just two or three breaks per hour, you actually will feel sharper and more creative, enabling you to be more productive and produce better work. I can't tell you how many of my best ideas and solutions came to me while taking a break and simply walking around and clearing my head.

Essential Oils and Other Essentials

You are probably thinking: *what do essential oils and aromatherapy have to do with self-esteem—especially the* repeat *aspect of the regime?* Quite a lot, actually!

It's as simple as this: the five senses are vital aspects of brain function, which in turn impact your overall health and well-being. The often-overlooked sense of smell is critical to other senses, such as taste, and has a dramatic influence on your mood and how you feel about yourself. If you are pooh-poohing this concept, think about what your mood would be like standing in a flower shop compared with being in the middle of a garbage dump.

Essential oils are accessible pretty much everywhere these days—including your local supermarket and drugstore—and you can even make many of them on your own. Most of them can be added to a warm bath, used in massage, or dabbed on the skin as a lotion to keep you feeling positive and relaxed throughout the day. A few cautionary notes: it is always a good idea to consult with your health care practitioner and/or dermatologist before applying (or ingesting) any oil, herb, or supplement. Be certain to follow the instructions on the packaging, and stop using it immediately if you notice any kind of allergic reaction, in which case you should immediately consult with your trusted physician.

I use essential oils on a regular basis and even make most of them myself so that I know exactly what's in them. I suggest a bit of experimentation initially to see which ones work best for you. There isn't a one-size-fits-all regimen, and there's something to be said for choosing the right essential oil to suit a particular mood on a given day. The secret is to determine which essential oils help you to relax and feel better about yourself. Once that has been established, *repeat, repeat, repeat!* Make your bath time part of your regular schedule two to three times a week when you know you won't be disturbed. This is your special private detoxification and relaxation time, and you deserve it!

These are the essential oils I recommend for boosting self-esteem and adding to your personal routine:

- *Bergamot*: Not only might the oil reduce stress, the supplement form may lower overall cholesterol and bad LDL cholesterol.
- *Cedarwood*: A woodsy scented oil that is believed to help with relaxation.
- *Eucalyptus*: Known for helping to curb symptoms of colds, flu, and other respiratory ailments.
- *Frankincense*: May yield anti-inflammatory benefits.
- *Jasmine*: Some people believe that jasmine can serve as both an antidepressant and as an aphrodisiac. Take your pick!

- *Lavender:* One of the most popular oils to help combat stress and anxiety.
- *Lemongrass:* Often used to alleviate inflammation and anxiety.
- *Patchouli:* Some practitioners believe this oil can treat skin conditions such as acne as well as relieve anxiety.
- *Peppermint:* Known to have properties that help alleviate digestive issues.
- *Rosemary:* Commonly used to stimulate brain function and increase concentration.
- *Sandalwood:* This scent is thought to relieve anxiety and lower blood pressure. Some people use sandalwood as an everyday air freshener.
- *Ylang-ylang:* Some research has shown that this oil boosts your mood. It also is effective at repelling certain insects.

As an alternative, sometimes I take Epsom salt baths for detoxification and to relax my muscles. I also surround myself with fragrant plants in my home and grow many of my own herbs. At the same time, I avoid products (detergents, soaps, etc.) that contain toxic chemicals and plastics (such as bottles), as they may contain toxins and release harmful polyvinyl chloride (PVC) into the environment during production.

Let's also not forget the importance of the sense of sound to our well-being and mental health. Sometimes, we need complete silence to relax and clear our heads of the day's problems and frustrations. Other times, music can soothe the savage beast within us. I like to listen to soft lounge music to create a calm and Zen-like atmosphere, but if jazz, hip-hop, classic rock, or heavy metal is your thing, by all means turn up the volume!

Whatever you incorporate into your routine, don't feel shy about mixing things up every now and then and trying something new. Something that works well for six months might become stale after a while—meaning your senses become immune to it like a cat overexposed to catnip—reducing its benefits. You want to feel fresh, energized, and confident after each repetition!

Affirmation: Mindfulness as Second Nature

I am mindful about the things I expose my body to.
I am mindful of the food and drink I ingest.
I am mindful about not allowing toxins and chemicals into my body.
I am mindful about relaxing all of my senses.
I am mindful about nurturing my mind, body, and soul.
I am mindful about continuing to educate myself about what works for my body and routines.
I am mindful that I must take time out for myself every now and then.

REview

- Create a daily routine that involves repeatable actions that work for you.
- Establish New Year's resolutions or monthly resolutions that involve strong motivators and reasonable rewards.
- Wake up one hour earlier each day to give yourself the gift of extra time to get things done.
- Give yourself a free pass if you slip up while establishing your desired routine.
- Watch what you eat and drink, as the things you put into your body influence how you feel about yourself.
- Exercise thirty minutes every day.
- Try to incorporate essential oils into your regime to help relax and alleviate stress.

CHAPTER NINE

~

REbound

A setback is a setup for a comeback.

—T. D. Jakes, bishop, author, and filmmaker

Didi Wong is the perfect example of a business professional who exemplifies the art of rebounding. Born in Hong Kong and schooled in England, she came to America to study at Boston University and to ultimately become a professional dancer, actress, and singer on Broadway. After graduation, she headed to the Big Apple to pursue her dream.

She feverishly auditioned for numerous roles but was passed over for one main reason: there simply weren't any juicy parts for Chinese dancer/actress/singers at that time.

Didi's parents urged her to return to Hong Kong to marry and assume the traditional role of housewife. She didn't want any part of that life and remained in New York, where she pivoted her career by applying her talents to other areas, such as public relations and catering. She networked her way to positions at Vera Wang, Pier59 Studios, and the New York Ballet. Although she excelled in all of her various roles and received temporary green cards, the pressure mounted for her to be sponsored by a company to gain permanent residence in the United States. Every time she left and returned to the United States, she was terrified that an immigration officer would stop her at the gate and deport her.

Unfortunately, despite Didi's tenacity, company sponsorship did not happen for a variety of reasons. Yet she refused to allow these setbacks to get in her way and repeatedly said "no" to her parents, who relentlessly continued to coerce her into moving to Hong Kong and assuming a proper Chinese lifestyle.

Just in the nick of time, Michael, her boyfriend of only six months, posed the question: "Do you want to get legal?" Her response: "Are you asking me to marry you?" He confirmed and she accepted the "proposal" on the spot.

Lo and behold, nearly two decades later, she and Michael now live happily in the United States—the Los Angeles area, to be exact—with their four kids. She may not have become a Broadway star, but she did realize her dream of being "on Broadway" as a keynote speaker. She even had the opportunity to sing onstage. She has deepened her roots in America, rebounded from her career setbacks, founded her own company—The Yes Academy—and became a successful keynote speaker, coach, angel investor, and TV/film producer. As if that's not enough, she is slated to be knighted in England by the Royal Order of Constantine the Great and St. Helen of Spain!

No matter where you may be in *The Self-Esteem REgime* process, setbacks, obstacles, conflicts, adversity, and difficulties are inevitable. In fact, I would go as far as saying they need to be *embraced*. Struggle must take place in order to create strength, character, and leadership. Most of all, you need to work your way through difficulties so that you may rebound and come out the other side stronger. Most heroes—from Odysseus in Homer's *Odyssey* to George Bailey (portrayed by Jimmy Stewart) in the film *It's a Wonderful Life* to Luke Skywalker (Mark Hamill) from the original *Star Wars* trilogy to Ripley (Sigourney Weaver in the *Alien* films)—must rebound from painful failure and/or loss in order to defeat their foes (no matter what form they make take). It's why we root for them in the first place! We like to see ourselves as fearless and courageous in the face of danger, finding the strength, courage, and fortitude to never give up on our goals and desires. If life were too easy and perfect, it would be boring and we would never have enough motivation to embark on our own quests and fulfill our dreams, whatever they may be.

Rebounding: A Critical Element to Success

How many times have you heard that a musician is making a "comeback album" or going on a "comeback tour"? It seems like Sir Paul McCartney of the Beatles, Wings, and solo artist fame—who has garnered more honors than any singer, musician, and songwriter in modern history and whose net worth is more than $1 billion—is making a "comeback album" with every new album release and sellout world tour.

No matter how big you may be—or think you are—there are always ways to fall from grace and drop from the spotlight. One major flop or scandal for a film actor or director could mean the end of his or her career. An injury to an all-star major league baseball player could signal the end of his athletic career. Or does it?

No matter whether one is a rock star, athlete, actress, or model, a successful rebound from adversity almost always seems like a tremendous accomplishment. In the case of a celebrity, it sometimes feels more exciting than the individual's initial rise to fame. Why, then, do the rest of us struggle so much with the concept of rebounding when it's so clearly essential to long-term success and self-esteem?

My personal path has never been a linear one, either. Being a professional model requires an enormous amount of resilience—before, during, and after one "makes it." I most certainly had my share of hard knocks and tumbles down the ladder—and *still* do. Each time this happens, I have found strategic ways to get right back up on my feet and rebound, which I cover as this chapter progresses.

While young and working in New York City's fashion district as a secretary in the early 1980s, I encountered many people who suggested that I become a model. They believed I had all of the necessary attributes. This was music to my ears—and more than enough encouragement for me to give it a try. I posed for test photography shots, which I then sent to famous modeling agencies in New York City. I decided to sign with Wilhelmina Models—one of the world's leading agencies—and was whisked off to Paris to gain essential experience for making it as a professional model. I knew this was my big shot—the one I had been dreaming of!

The one thing I didn't factor into the equation? That I would become homesick. I was twenty-one, alone in a foreign country, I didn't speak French, and I had no friends. Don't get me wrong, Paris was fabulous—but the luster wears off in a hurry when you're feeling despondent and wondering whether you are good enough. After one year and a few jobs, I returned to New York City without having "made it," as I'd hoped. Once again, I returned to working as a temp secretary. My self-esteem plummeted.

Dominating Your Daily Demons

Maya Angelou famously said, "Hoping for the best, prepared for the worst, and unsurprised by anything in between." This is so true! Emblazon her statement in your journal or prominently on your desk.

You never want to be negative and predict that something bad will happen. It's not just superstitious to do that, but it predisposes you toward that result and you may end up making that a reality. Instead, *hope* that good things will happen and place all of your effort and psychological energy into it. At the same time, it's always good to have a plan B ready and waiting—just in case things go off course. This way, you won't be unsurprised if something happens and you won't feel the sting quite as much. Life can be unpredictable and there is no such thing as "good luck" or "bad luck"; there is only *the luck you make.*

Now, here's the kicker! My first job back in the States happened to be located in the C-Suite top floor of Revlon cosmetics. At work each day, I couldn't help but notice that the walls were adorned with oversized posters of glamorous Revlon models. Boy, was I angry at myself! I'd given up, even though I knew that the girls on the walls didn't look that different from me. Deep down, underneath all of the self-pity, I believed I had what it took.

I became more determined than ever to succeed. I saved up enough money from my job at Revlon to buy a roundtrip ticket to Europe. This time, I ventured to Milan, Italy, where I had a new modeling agency lined up.

I was 100 percent ready, and nothing was going to stop me this time! Modeling is a career rife with rejection, so I had to learn how to buck up and not take it personally. I channeled the anger and disappointment from my France experience into honing my modeling skills, including my runway walking technique and posing for the camera.

Going to Italy and giving modeling another shot turned out to be the best decision I ever made. I felt at home there, I learned the language, and I made immediate friendships. After some trial and error, I landed enough modeling gigs to create my print portfolio, build my reputation, and earn steady income. I was on my way! But I can confidently say that I would not have made it in Italy if I hadn't been forced to rebound from my unsuccessful year in France.

Rebounding on and off the Court

Whether rebounding from a relationship ending or a career setback, the mind-set is the same and parallels the physical act of rebounding in the sport of basketball. When the basketball is thrown up in the air by a player on either team but misses the hoop, everyone's objective is to *get the rebound*. Boiled down, what is happening here? Everyone is trying to take advantage of the miss, including (perhaps *especially*) the person who didn't sink the basket. Note that this athlete and his or her teammates do not stop to sulk or lay blame. *They aggressively go after the rebound.*

The same may be applied to all areas of your life. You must always grab the next opportunity after a setback—even a small one, as we soon explore—or someone else will get a clear-cut advantage, and then you'll feel even worse than before, your losses unnecessarily compounding.

We all know people who failed in their first jobs . . . and their second . . . and even their third. Some were laid off. Others may have lost their positions due to poor job performance. This can feel so demeaning! The natural reaction is to blame oneself: *What did I do wrong? I must be a total failure. I'm a screwup. I can't do anything right. Who would want to hire me after all of that history?*

The result of such thinking is to fall prey to denial, frustration, and self-doubt. This is the exact opposite of what you should do. Instead, visualize that you are on a basketball court and missed a basket. "So what?" you tell yourself. "My job now is to jump up and *grab the rebound!*"

Clarissa's Corner

Michael Jordan, perhaps the greatest National Basketball Association (NBA) star of all time, once made a stunning commercial in which he confessed some of his failures during his years on the court: "I have missed more than nine thousand shots in my career. I have lost almost three hundred games. On twenty-six occasions I have been entrusted to take the game-winning shot . . . and missed. And I have failed over and over again in my life. And that is why I succeed."

That is truly remarkable! But why wasn't the great Michael Jordan boasting about his accomplishments instead?

It wasn't about modesty, although Jordan does, in fact, seem to be a humble man. He homed in on his failures in order to show others that everyone makes many mistakes—including himself—and that he strives to become a better athlete by paying attention to these mind-blowing statistics that no one else ever noticed.

The main thing is that Jordan never succumbed to self-doubt and frustration. He trotted right back out on the court and played his heart out. As if that's not enough, Jordan's switch to the baseball diamond may have been a bust, but it didn't stop him from later returning to full glory back on the NBA court.

Didi Wong, whose story was mentioned at the beginning of this chapter, is an all-star rebounder. She did not sulk when she hit brick walls as an actress, dancer, and singer. She didn't blame anyone—including herself—for her unfortunate situation. She didn't regret having tried to pursue her Broadway dream.

Instead, Didi reassessed her strengths, pivoted, and leapt for the rebound. She mined the connections she had in order to shift from the worlds of film, theater, and dance and to create and establish a unique role for herself as a keynote speaker, coach, and entrepreneur. She cheerfully pressed on to succeed in her new endeavors with fierce determination.

On a less dramatic scale, my friend Peter is a virtuoso guitarist. No one practiced more hours a day than Peter. If you heard him play his instrument, you would think he was a Carnegie Hall–caliber performer.

Unfortunately, his efforts as a recording artist and live performer never panned out. He couldn't make a living with his beloved instrument. Peter refused to give in. He went back to college and earned a bachelor's degree in accounting, followed by CPA certification. He applied to financial and accounting positions in several firms until he landed a solid position. This may seem like a major compromise for him and perhaps even drudgery for someone who longed to be a musician. Not so! The company he worked for exclusively handled money management for A-list musicians, which meant he would still be involved in the music industry on some level and feel connected to his passion.

The Seven Keys to Rebounding

The most resilient people—like Didi Wong—understand and implement the seven keys to rebounding:

1. *Acknowledge the problem*: It may be easy to identify what happened—that is, losing a job, missing a revenue target in your business, damaging a relationship—but it's much more difficult to *own up to it*. Denial of a situation only worsens things, preventing you from searching for solutions and increasing your self-doubt. It may be scary and painful to accept a certain problem—but denying it might be even more costly in terms of wasting precious time or increasing and/or prolonging feelings of anxiety and self-pity.

2. *Seek industry counsel*: Such a person could be a knowledgeable coach, friend, or former colleague. The idea here is to identify someone who can relate to your experience and share his or her wisdom. There is a good chance this individual will make you feel better simply by saying, "Don't beat up on yourself. I've been there many times." I have a friend who shared his extreme work anxiety with his longtime mentor, who had been a giant in her industry. The mentor admitted to having had similar issues and being prescribed antidepressants by a psychologist, which helped her to get through a difficult, high-pressure time in her career. Knowing that someone who was as wise, experienced, and

confident as his mentor had similar experiences eased the situation for my friend.

3. *Confide in someone you trust:* This one may be complicated. You do not necessarily want to spill your guts to every friend, relative, or former colleague, as you don't know where your private thoughts and feelings will go. The person with whom you share your setback must be someone you trust with confidential information and who is a superb listener, won't judge you, and can resist offering you unsolicited advice. The benefit of someone who fits this description is that you feel catharsis: you can unload your pain and anxieties in a safe space. Once you do so, you'll feel better right away and then those emotions won't spill out into other areas of your life (including anger toward other people). A word of caution: try not to overdo the drama, if possible, and don't barrage your confidante more than once a week. After a while, such repeated sharing can be grating and unproductive. Even your ardent fans who sincerely want to help you need a break and may secretly think you are whining.

4. *Identify the root cause:* Once you have come to terms with your dilemma, you do want to take a good, hard look in the mirror and assess what went wrong. The idea is to distinguish whether: (A) you were not at fault, because it was beyond your control; (B) you may have had at least a partial role in what went awry; or (C) a combination of A and B.

5. *Learn a relevant lesson:* There are lessons to be gleaned from A, B, and C in number 4 above. If it's A, you can shrug your shoulders and move on. If it's B, learn from your mistake, identify ways to avoid repeating it, and press forward. If it's C, the same answer as B applies, except that you have more work to do to improve before you can move forward. Whether it's A, B, or C, ask yourself whether or not this has been a repetitive pattern in your life and career. If it's occurred more than once, you may have a deeper concern to resolve.

6. *Take a reasonable amount of time off:* Everyone needs some head-clearing every now and then. Once you've sorted out the root cause of your issue, make a note of it in your journal and then distance yourself from it for a bit. If you've had a traumatic ex-

perience with your boss at your last company, for example, it's going to be extra hard to confidently jump straight back into the work fray. Take a few days off—or even a couple of weeks, if you can—to unwind. Do something fun that is completed unrelated to what went wrong. You will find yourself stronger, replenished, and more capable of facing whatever might be coming your way.

7. *Rebound!* This is where many people tend to get stuck. Things start to derail in your mind when you set your expectations for getting back on track too high. Let's go back to a basketball rebound: all you want to do at this point in the game is to jump up and grab the ball when the throw misses its mark and caroms off the backboard. In other words, a rebound is *one simple action.* You are (hopefully) not just reacting by closing your eyes with the ball clutched in your hands and making a wild throw across the court at the basket (unless the game is in its final seconds, of course). You should feel good about holding the ball, as you have accomplished a small goal and now have various options: you can leisurely dribble; pass to a teammate; or dribble down the court to pass, make a layup, or even dunk one in the net.

Similarly, when rebounding from a setback, you want to think in terms of an easily attainable goal. If, for example, you lost your job, you might spruce up your résumé. When that is completed, you can check it off—*done!* You've made a rebound and have jump-started your *career* rebound. If you happen to have gone through a relationship breakup and enough time has elapsed, you can start investigating reputable dating sites. The goal is not to go all-out and initiate a serious relationship too quickly, because then you risk another connotation of the word *rebound,* as in diving in too soon before being completely over a former partner.

Be Kind to Yourself

I can't emphasize this enough: no matter what trial or tribulation you are going through, no matter how much you might think you screwed up, *be kind to yourself!* When things don't turn out as planned, you need to be forgiving of any mistakes in order to persevere and get back on track without missing a beat. There is zero benefit to beating yourself up; you will feel worse and hinder your ability to rebound. As stated earlier in the chapter, make this a teachable moment for next time and then move on.

There may be people out there who will make you feel bad enough—whether well-intentioned or not—so don't add to your mind chatter by playing your own internal blame game. Friends, family, and former colleagues may shoot you down the moment you are taking the rebound, that fragile first step toward regaining your footing. In my case, although there were some people who were supportive and encouraging when I headed off to Italy, there were also those who said unhelpful things like "Isn't it really hard to break in?"; "Well, remember what happened last time in Paris"; and "Isn't it a one-in-a-million shot?"

Guess what I did? I ignored all of them and set off on my merry way to Italy!

Clar-ion Call

When we feel disappointment in ourselves and lousy, we tend to punish ourselves even more, so that we *look the part of the victim*. We dress in frumpy clothes, we binge on junk food, and we stay up all night watching mindless infomercials. Some women (and men, too!) don't change their clothes, shower, or brush their teeth or hair. This kind of pity party accomplishes absolutely nothing, except making you feel more despondent.

As I've mentioned throughout the regime, you often become the person you reflect to the outside world—whether it's a positive or negative persona. If you look and/or act like a wounded animal, you risk internalizing and externalizing that, and then people will regard you as if you are less than the shining star you have the potential to become.

The solution? Reward yourself. Don't think of it in terms of validating a setback, but rather, a pick-me-up to brighten your world.

Replenish yourself with something that makes you feel and look good. Get a massage or a makeover. Buy a new dress. If money is an issue, something as price conscious as an accessory (such as a bracelet, pendant, scarf, hat, or scrunchie) can help add that extra bounce to your rebound.

It's crucial that you toss all of those unsupportive comments right out the window or self-doubt may cause you to falter. In order to believe in yourself, you must be kind to yourself and not listen to pointless negative drivel. You must always treat yourself well—mind, body, and spirit—in order to function well and turn that rebound into a successful comeback.

Affirmation: I Will Never Falter

The universe is preparing me for my greatest comeback.
I will find the solution to any obstacle that stands in my way.
In a negative situation, I will always find a positive way out.
As always, I will stay committed to my self-care.
I will commit to getting at least seven hours of restorative sleep.
No person, situation, or thing will hinder my positive outcome.
The boundaries I set for myself are clear, concise, and understood by all.
I will remain productive in setting and achieving my goals on a daily basis.
I will never falter in accomplishing my tasks in a timely manner.

REview

- Recognize that it's entirely possible to progress several steps forward in the regime, regress backward, and then need to rebound in order to move forward.
- Think of the word *rebound* in terms of the basketball connotation: when you are faced with a setback, "jump up" and accomplish one small thing that propels you toward your next step.
- Understand and implement the seven keys to rebounding.
- Be kind to yourself!
- Reward yourself after minor or major disappointments, even though it may seem counterintuitive.

CHAPTER TEN

~

REdirect

Character is doing the right thing when nobody is looking.

—J. C. Watts, clergyman and politician

Felicia, a young woman I know, is struggling to turn a corner after having successfully rebounded from several personal and professional setbacks. Although part of her feels she is back on track, something seems missing deep inside. She can hardly put into words what she is feeling; she only knows that people still aren't responding to her the way she would like.

When I ask her for specific examples of what she is experiencing, this is what she conveys:

Case #1: "There's my coworker Marla. . . . I guess she still holds a grudge because while I was at my low point, I didn't have the strength to back her up at a team meeting."

Case #2: "My friend Susan doesn't seem to get why I couldn't call her back all those weeks. I was in such a funk I really couldn't face some people."

Case #3: "My sister Mara—well, I love her, but she can be such a bitch. She's just jealous that our Dad took me out to lunch for my birthday because he knew I was struggling and wanted to help. He's never taken her out to lunch—she's jealous and thinks that's my fault."

Case #4: "My mentor, Ron—he's upset about nothing. He gave me a book to read to help me through my rough patch. I read and enjoyed the book very much. I was a bit short on money so, when I was done, I sold it on eBay. Ron called a few days later to see how I was doing. He seemed pleased to hear that I had rebounded. Then, out of nowhere, he asked if he could have the book back, as it had sentimental value for him. Oops! I didn't know what to say, except apologize and tell a little white lie—that I lost it on the subway. He hasn't returned my calls and emails since, even though I bought him a replacement copy of the book. It seems unfair, especially because I still need him as my mentor."

Felicia doesn't understand what, if anything, she has done wrong in these scenarios and how she can repair her relationships.

I admit it right off the bat: I am totally old school when it comes to manners and being an upright citizen in all areas of one's life. It's not a religious or moral dictum, it's simply what is required of us as human beings—for ourselves, as well as others. A lot of things get taken for granted these days, especially in terms of how we treat one another when we are experiencing a personal low. When we are frustrated and disappointed, we feel we have a carte blanche excuse to assign blame, take our anger out on others, and show our worst selves to the outside world.

I believe character is everything when it comes to building and retaining self-esteem. Though we all have strengths and weaknesses in this regard, we also have our individual blind spots, which is why it is so important to look at ourselves objectively from all angles. When character lapses occur, we must learn how to redirect our behaviors to align with how we wish to be perceived and respected by others.

Felicia, the woman referenced in the story above, is a good-hearted, well-meaning person who happens to be an introvert. I can attest to the fact that she genuinely loves the people she seems to have distanced. I empathize with what she had to undergo to rebound and get back on her feet—and I am happy she followed the regime to accomplish this. She is not at all what I would consider a selfish person. Unfortunately, while building herself back up, she lost her way in terms of certain aspects of her character. She is unable to see through her own blinders of pain and suffering to recognize that she is falling short in her interactions with the people she loves and respects. She doesn't realize that the best way to fully regain her footing is to give back to the people who helped her while she was down.

Now is the time for her to redirect her behaviors in order to become a whole person again, prove she still has integrity to the people in her circle, and help restore even more of her self-confidence.

Redirect Your Best Self

One of the greatest measures of character is the way you make people feel when they interact with you. When was the last time you did something nice for someone without an expectation of anything in return? You just did it and forgot it. This may take the form of something as simple as holding the elevator doors open for someone who is running to get inside or helping a woman carry a stroller up and down subway stairs.

Let me restate this: Felicia is not a bad person or a person of bad character. She simply needs to redirect the things she already knows deep inside and then relay them back to the world. Here are some of her missteps:

- *Case #1, coworker Marla*: There is no excuse—not even being at low ebb—for failing to have a team member's back. We all have a responsibility to take care of our own.
- *Case #2, friend Susan*: Shutting out friends is also not beneficial to anyone, even introverts. All Felicia needed to do was call her friend and explain that she was going through a rough patch and may be a bit reclusive while she figures some things out. A good friend would have been nonjudgmental, tried to help her get through the situation, and given her necessary space on request.
- *Case #3, sister Mara*: Felicia needs to put herself in Mara's shoes! Although it's not her fault that her father may seem at times to favor her over her sister—and remember, this is all subjective, depending on one's point of view—it can still feel hurtful. Instead of considering her sister a "bitch," Felicia could have invited her sister to the lunch and/or gently suggested her father extend a separate lunch invitation to Mara at some point.

- *Case #4, mentor Ron:* There is an old expression that goes something like this: "One should return a five-pound bag of sugar for every cup borrowed." (A variant of this is "Borrow a car and return it with a full tank of gas.") Felicia needed to return the favor with the purchase of something special for her mentor (perhaps a different book). Not only should she have been 100 percent certain that her mentor had *gifted* her the book—not *loaned* it—before doing anything as aggressive as selling it on eBay. The worst part of it? She didn't come clean and tell the truth to her mentor about what she had done with the book. Ron may have seen through her little white lie and decided loaning the book to Felicia was his last kind gesture to her.

Actions speak louder than words. Below are just a few specific ways you can redirect your strong character toward others and, in turn, yourself in daily interaction:

- Penning a personalized, handwritten thank-you or apology note.
- Compliment him or her on a job well done.
- Remember to express thanks to someone who offers help or assistance, even if you decide not to follow the advice.
- Perform an unexpected favor for a person who does something kind to you.
- Make a donation in the name of a person you feel has done something generous for you.

Finally, always wish the best for others—even if it's someone with whom you are competitive. Your intent should be to see others succeed and be happy for them. When your heart is full in this way, there is no room for jealousy. The universe is filled with abundance and there is plenty of success to go around. Character is not something that is hanging in your closet or parked inside your garage. It's the way you think and interact with those around you.

Every day, ask yourself: *Did I make someone feel good about herself today?*

Try it! It's the perfect self-esteem boost for both of you.

Dominating Your Daily Demons

If you really want to offer a sincere thank-you to someone or to extend an apology for a misstep, a handwritten snail mail note is the perfect solution.

You're probably thinking: *Clarissa, are you nuts? Who uses snail mail anymore?*

The fact that communication through technology—texts, emails, social media—has overtaken our lives is *precisely* why you need to put pen to paper. Digital exchanges are way too easy and seem like a superficial quick fix. The rarity of receiving a handwritten letter makes the recipient feel as if the effort was personal and sincere, as it took more time and energy to produce. Not only that, as you have experienced from your daily journaling, it's cathartic to write things down to express your emotions.

Essential Character Traits for Good Self-Esteem

As stated earlier, we all have our character strengths and our weaknesses. We should consider ourselves works in progress and on a never-ending journey of self-improvement. Without a doubt, you possess many admirable character traits. Your goal is to self-reflect in order to identify which among the following character traits require redirection:

1. *Be honest*: Don't deceive, cheat, steal, or lie. Even a little white lie can be damaging, as we learned from Felicia's behavior.
2. *Be reliable*: Do what you say you'll do. I mentioned in prior chapters, for example, that being tardy becomes a stain attached to you that is difficult to remove.
3. *Be courageous*: Have the courage to do the right thing. J. C. Watts's quote that opens this chapter says it all. Being brave against tough obstacles may pose some risk to you, but doing the right thing feels good and boosts self-esteem.
4. *Be compassionate*: Treat those who are in unfortunate situations with sympathy and understanding. I know many people who have suffered a great deal in recent years. You should not view

it as "political" to offer a helping hand through donations and volunteering—it's just being a good human being.

5. *Be loyal*: Stand by your family, friends, colleagues, and country. Disagreements may occur, but these loved ones will unconditionally have your back in times of need.

6. *Be adaptable*: Take life as it comes—whether events are good, bad, or somewhere in the middle. If you regard yourself as an adaptable person, you will be better prepared to handle curveballs when they are thrown at you.

7. *Be respectful*: Treat people as you wish to be treated. This also includes how you speak to others; derogatory remarks of any kind are not acceptable.

8. *Be patient*: Like all clichés, "good things come to those who wait" holds a great deal of truth. Would you rather stand in a long line with someone who bellyaches about the wait—or a person who tells amusing anecdotes?

9. *Be level headed*: Try not to overdramatize. We all know our share of "drama mamas" who exaggerate everything and act as if the sky is falling all the time. Doing this for comic effect once in a while is one thing but behaving this way to garner excessive attention and/or sympathy can grate on people's nerves.

10. *Be generous*: This can refer to offers of time, money, or advice or even sharing credit for an accomplishment. This overlaps with item 4 but is worth specifically mentioning. Actions speak louder than words!

11. *Be optimistic*: No one likes being around someone who is negative. In his wonderful best-selling book, *A Complaint-Free World*, author Will Bowen espouses the benefits of *not* complaining. He even offers a challenge anyone can tackle to ensure a life of positivity!

12. *Be graceful*: Handle setbacks and losses—as well as successes— with finesse. Everyone loves to witness good sportsmanship! In January 2021, after Tom Brady's Tampa Bay Buccaneers defeated Drew Brees's New Orleans Saints in a do-or-die playoff game, the winning quarterback went back on the football field and threw touchdowns to his opponent's son. Now *that* is class!

13. *Be accessible*: Everyone requires a certain amount of downtime, but you also need to be available to people in your community. Whether you are introverted or not, take the time—beyond just texts and emails—to truly pay attention to the important people in your life.

Meet People Where They Are

It's just a fact of life that there are people who are going to disappoint us, no matter how inadvertent their action (or inaction) might be. In many cases, you'll probably find that the individuals you are struggling to get along with are experiencing some measure of self-doubt, just like you.

Earlier in this chapter, I stated that Felicia needed to put herself in Mara's shoes. We should always do this when we face an opposing viewpoint. Sometimes we are at a total loss to figure out why someone was insulted or hurt by something we said. The natural response is along the lines of "Oh, she's overreacting" or "Come on, you know that's not what I meant."

Let's face it: we all get annoyed with or disappointed by *everyone* at *some point*. Your brother may be terrible at remembering special family events. Your mother may never be capable of giving you a compliment that doesn't have a sharp double edge to it. Your best friend may never reciprocate a birthday lunch, even though you've graciously treated for years.

Your charge is to consider redirecting how and where you meet people, even if they happen to display certain shortcomings. There is always a place where you can greet them in the middle and accept them for who and what they are. Sometimes, what you are receiving is indeed the best they can give—and that is okay!

If, for example, your brother always needs a gentle reminder about his young nephew's birthday, so be it. Once he's aware of it and buys the child a late birthday present, all is forgiven. If your mother tells you, "My granddaughter looks like she dressed herself today," don't presume she means that you dress your child poorly; perhaps she meant it as a compliment to the child for completing the task herself. If your seemingly ungenerous friend who never treats you to a birthday lunch spends time on the phone listening to you vent about your boss, thank her profusely for it, as that may be an even more sincere and valuable gesture of friendship than paying for your birthday lunch.

In all likelihood, there are plausible reasons why these folks behave in the ways they do. Don't assume the worst. Give them the benefit of the doubt! Your forgetful brother may just have a poor memory for birthdays. Your mother may not have a clue how to offer a sincere compliment, given how her mother and father treated her. Your friend may be too embarrassed to admit she is struggling financially and can't afford to pay for your birthday lunch.

Clar-ion Call

Overreacting to what people say to you is probably an indicator that you are still struggling with a self-esteem issue. If you snap every time someone says something to you, people will regard you as being defensive and/or hypersensitive.

The way to avoid these reactions when you believe someone is insulting you is to step back, take a deep breath, smile politely, and say in a level voice, "Oh, thanks—I never thought of it that way." Then calmly walk away.

Your statement leaves the other person deliberating about her own intention, rather than focusing on your reaction. Whatever her initial intent might have been, you will notice a tonal shift and/or rephrase the next time she addresses you.

The explanations above are not to make excuses for anyone's shortcomings, but, rather, to meet him or her halfway. It's not up to you to judge the other person's reaction. It may be impossible to change his or her personality or behaviors, in any regard. The point is that, in order to demonstrate strong character, you must automatically presume the *best* of intentions and take things at face value. Instead of jumping to a conclusion, consider the notion that, if someone is angry, irritated, or hurt by something you said or did, you should step into her shoes and redirect your thoughts to presume there was something to her reaction. In all likelihood, you'll realize that you were at least *partially* to blame for the situation, even if it was a simple misunderstanding that has occurred. Sometimes taking the high road and accepting partial blame is the best way to move forward with a secure, valuable relationship.

Humility Is Underrated

As a former actress and model, I've been up against some egos larger than Mount Rushmore. Braggarts are a turnoff, no matter who they are, what they have accomplished, how much money they have, or how beautiful they are. Your interactions with other people say a great deal about your character and the type of individual you are.

I know one usually sweet, caring man who acts like a complete jerk to waiters and waitresses in restaurants. He barks orders the minute he sits down, asking unrelenting questions about the menu and giving detailed instructions about his order: serving foods "extra hot" or "extra cold," or in a certain order, or with various accompaniments served on the side. If anything in his order is the slightest bit off, he sends it right back with an insult and expects a discount, if not a complete freebie. Of course, everyone has a right to receive food the way he or she wants it and to expect quality food and service. However, I find this man's dismissive tone with servers to be condescending and embarrassing.

Humility is a positive attribute under any circumstance. How well you treat waiters, Uber drivers, receptionists, plumbers, hairstylists, and anyone else in service is *a reflection on you.* There is nothing weak about being humble and treating other people as equals and with respect. Any feeling of superiority you may have toward others generally means that you are *insecure about yourself.* If anything, service workers demand greater respect and courtesy, as their jobs tend to be physically (and emotionally) demanding. They also may have received some form of abuse throughout the day from other customers and may not even be at fault for whatever bad experience you believe you endured.

Every time someone has performed a paid service for you, redirect your appreciation afterward with a look straight in the eye and a sincere thank-you. If you must express dissatisfaction about something, handle it courteously and in a gentle tone of voice. That worker will be sure to take your concerns more seriously if you treat her with respect. And the next time you arrive in that restaurant, the manager and the waitstaff will roll out the red carpet for you!

Clarissa's Corner

If you truly seek to redirect your character, here is a small tip that takes very little effort but goes a long way.

When a restaurant server does an exceptional job—for example, getting a difficult order right, bringing out the food and/or drinks in timely fashion, offering extra napkins when unsolicited, and so forth—request to speak to the manager. When she approaches with that "Uh-oh, what went wrong now?" look and asks, "How may I help you?" smile and say, "I just have to tell you—my table server was excellent. He was charming, brought out the food lightning fast, and was always there for us before we had to look around for him. That guy is a keeper. I'll be back here, for sure! Thank you so much."

The manager will be staring at your back as you leave and scratching her head for a while. But when she passes on the compliment to her waiter, you can be assured that both will be beaming from ear to ear!

Immediate Redirects That Improve Self-Esteem

There is a wide variety of other things you can do to redirect your thoughts and feel better about yourself and be more confident. The overarching change is to break free of any preconceived notions you have of the person you are, how you to choose to behave with others, and how you occupy your time. You have control over all these areas, so you want to strive to be the best you can be at all times.

Redirect Your Relationships

If you are struggling to work out issues with someone—a friend, family member, colleague at work, and so forth—focus your thoughts more on her and less about yourself. Demonstrate genuine interest and concern for the other person. Few disputes are worth ending a relationship. If you can't come to terms, agree to disagree and never bring up sore subjects again.

Redirect an Escalating Conversation

So many disagreements are avoidable, if only both parties utilized the right tools of expression. You don't always have to win an argument and you certainly shouldn't be arguing for argument's sake. An accusatory phrase such as "You always do that!" will be perceived as aggressive, which already escalates the volume in a conversation.

I know, sometimes emotions run high in the heat of the moment. It can be difficult to lower your own temperature once you have become riled up, no matter who is to blame. Here is the problem: emotions are never interpreted the way you expect or want them to be, and it's hard to take them back once they are released in the open. If you scream, rant, complain, or even cry, the other person may become increasingly angry or frustrated. It takes strength of character and willpower to calm yourself when your buttons have been pushed.

In order to de-escalate a charged exchange, try responding with kind words. A sincere compliment—that cannot be interpreted as sarcasm or condescension—will be a powerful countermeasure against hostility. For example, instead of shouting something defensive like "You always tell me I assemble things wrong!"—which immediately irritates the other party—say something along the lines of "You know your stuff when it comes to assembling things, and I appreciate you offering to help, but this time I would prefer to try to do it on my own. If I fail, I fail."

If the disagreement continues, practice active listening: strong eye contact without interruption while the other individual is speaking, and when you respond, say "I hear you" and repeat back what has been said in order to ensure that you interpreted the message correctly. You still may not see completely eye to eye—especially if the subject is politics!—but at least she knows that you respect her point of view and still care about her.

Redirect Your Fear

Unless you are in a genuine fight-or-flight situation—you or someone else's life is in imminent, physical jeopardy—fight your fear! Being frightened about little things only adds more stress and anxiety in your life, releasing too much adrenaline in your body that may potentially cause issues such as muscle spasms, high blood pressure, sleeplessness, depression, and a host of other ailments. Any and all of these problems can worsen self-esteem.

How does one deal with fear? Many excellent books—such as *Fear Is Fuel* by Patrick J. Sweeney II—have been written about the subject and, unfortunately, I don't have the space here to cover them all in detail. However, I do have three surefire ways to help ease the amount of fear in your life: yoga, meditation, and aerobic exercise (such as biking and jogging).

Redirect by Challenging Yourself

It's never too late to try to challenge yourself by doing something you never thought you would do—or assumed that you *couldn't* do. I once jumped out of a plane on *L'Isola dei Famosi* (*The Celebrity Island* or *The Island of the Famous*), the Italian equivalent of the U.S. reality TV show *Survivor*.

If you are stuck in any of the stages of the regime, try to redirect yourself by trying something new. It doesn't necessarily have to be life threatening and terrifying; it's simply a way of showing how much you can accomplish. See if any of these are on your bucket list of things to attempt: performing stand-up comedy; singing publicly; submitting a book proposal to a literary agent or editor for consideration; jet-skiing; parasailing; hot air ballooning; mountain hiking; bungee jumping; and so on.

Redirect your *can'ts* into *can do's* today!

Redirect Your informational Input

Who or what are you listening to? With the prevalence of digital media, you have virtually unlimited access to entertainment of all kinds: books, music, podcasts, TV shows, films, blogs, magazines, newspapers, and on and on. Make a conscious effort to fill your senses with positive, happy, and healthy inputs. If the TV news you watch every morning and evening depresses or enrages you, flip the channel! No one is forcing you to continue to watch things that upset you. Instead, redirect!

Affirmation: Redirecting Character

I respect everyone—whether I understand them or not.
I am a person of strength and good character.
I have a serving heart and help humanity in any way I can.
I turn every negative thought into a positive one.
I insist on honesty and integrity from myself.
I assume the best intentions of other people.
I recognize that common sense prevails when all else fails.

REview

- Redirect your behaviors in order to demonstrate that you are a person of strong character.
- Meet people halfway when they seem unable to fulfill your expectations of them.
- Recognize your character strengths and weaknesses and strive toward improving the latter.
- Be a humble, generous, compassionate person, as these character traits will make others feel good and, in turn, boost your self-esteem.
- Treat everyone with respect at all times.
- Redirect your relationships, conversations, fears, and self-imposed limitations to generate more positive outcomes.

CHAPTER ELEVEN

~

REspect

Respect yourself and others will respect you.

—Confucius, Chinese philosopher

Heidi, a successful attorney in her forties, has had it with her parents and vows to never see—or even speak to—them again. Let's dive into the sad backstory of this scenario, which is all too common.

Ultrareligious and conservative in their views, Heidi's parents had always been outspoken against interracial, interfaith, and same-sex marriages. After years of concealing her sexual orientation from them, Heidi finally revealed her love for Shelley, her partner. Her parents shrugged it off, refusing to take the relationship seriously. They considered it a phase and continued to set their daughter up on blind dates with men, which Heidi declined.

One day, Heidi went to her parent's house for her first dinner with Shelley as a guest. It was tense but generally fine until Heidi clinked her glass, rose, and announced that she and her partner were getting married. Things escalated quickly from there. Her mother began to sob. Her father said they were living in sin and threatened to disown her and remove her from their will. Heidi reacted to her parents' outburst by screaming and cursing at them, pounding her fists on the table, and calling them "homophobic bigots." Shelley, upset by the outbursts, excused herself and fled in tears.

Weeks went by. . . .

Heidi and Shelley have arranged for a small private wedding with only their closest accepting friends and relatives. Heidi has not said a word to either parent since that fateful night, ignoring their phone calls, texts, and emails. It goes without saying that they were not invited to the wedding.

The morning of the wedding, Shelley approaches Heidi and begs her to call her parents, make amends, and extend a last-minute invitation to them.

"Are you kidding? The way they treated us?!" Heidi flares. "I won't ever forgive them for the way they spoke to you—to us. Even if they manage to apologize and show up, I know how they truly feel. They do not respect us—and never will."

"But," Shelley implored, holding her future spouse's hand, "How do you really know that? Have you given them the slightest chance to explain—maybe apologize? I see how this whole thing is hurting you every single day, Heidi. I can see your anger and guilt—it's even impacting your work at the law firm."

"It's way too late," Heidi dismissed. "They blew it. Since they don't respect us, I don't respect them. I'm done!"

What's the single most important thing you can give to someone else and to yourself?

R-E-S-P-E-C-T!

Heidi's tale is all too common these days. I am not going to choose a side in this unwinnable dispute or pass any moral, ethical, or religious judgment on either party. They are both right and they are both wrong, and that is the dilemma much of the world faces every single day—differing viewpoints among religions, ethnic groups, genders, countries, political parties, and on and on.

We are never going to agree on everything. A utopia is simply not possible—at least not in the foreseeable future. And yet—is Heidi's rigid position worth digging in when she has no clue about how her parents had reacted in the ensuing weeks leading up to the wedding? Is it worth alienating her parents forever?

Heidi can't see past being hurt and offended in order to give her parents a chance to cool off, think things through, and possibly come around enough to restore civility and work together to figure things out. They probably wouldn't be completely accepting and joyous or offer their blessing on the nuptials, but maybe they would budge *just enough* to avoid permanently fracturing the family.

In the same way Heidi's parents failed to respect their daughter and her partner's lifestyle, Heidi disrespected them right back with a vengeance. Her reactive behavior didn't accomplish anything, nor did her subsequent shutdown to her parents' attempts at reconciliation. When one demonstrates a lack of respect to others—as in the case of Heidi and her parents—*self*-respect diminishes—and so does self-esteem for all parties involved.

Goodwill, Grace, and Glory

I make no pretense that I can snap my fingers and end global hunger, create world peace, or turn Heidi and her family into a harmonious Great American Family. What I can offer, however, are tools to help Heidi get past her emotions—which I do not dismiss—and win back her parents' respect by demonstrating respect to them. Heidi has every right to be distraught over her parents' outburst; however, her counterattack wasn't any better. Why? Because we must *always* respect other human beings—most especially our parents.

We don't have to *agree*, mind you, but rather dig deep within ourselves to find inner strength and tap into goodwill, grace, and glory for the greater good. We must accept people for who and what they are, find some area of common ground, and move on as best we can to live in harmony.

Heidi, for example, might have been better served if she had simmered down at the dinner and allowed a few days to pass to enable everyone to cool down and have a serious, calm discussion. Clearly, her parents needed some time to process and adjust to the news of the wedding. It's then—and *only then*—that Heidi would have an opportunity to reason with her parents—either by phone or, even better, face to face (*not* by text or email, which is too impersonal and subject to miscommunication). The chance of success may be slim, but isn't it worth it to save one's family ties? The longer their last interaction stands and the wedding day fast approaches, the greater the division grows between them.

Heidi would enter this crucial conversation with her parents with an open heart and mind. Her tone should be respectful, as well as calm, gentle, and nonjudgmental, as she says something along the lines of:

Heidi: Mom, Dad . . . I know the news of the wedding was something of a shock to you . . .
[*Note that she is acknowledging their feelings.*]

Heidi: I didn't mean to upset either of you. I love you both.
[*Note that this is a major olive branch, but not a concession of any ideology. She's not agreeing with her parents; she simply states two important truths that can bond them: her parents were upset, and she does love them.*]

At this stage, her parents might be so appreciative of their daughter's respectful approach that they, in turn, show respect to her:

Mom: We love you, too, dear. . . .

Dad: Yes . . . it was a lot for us to take in. I admit, I may have over-reacted a bit.

Aha—a slight concession! Although not exactly an apology, it's a clear sign that both parents admit to *some* responsibility for what happened. Healing can begin because both parties respect each other. At this point, Heidi might invite her parents to attend the wedding. They have the opportunity to decide whether to show up and support their daughter or not; it's completely their decision.

Dominating Your Daily Demons

Whether you are the parent or the adult child caught in a disagreement, respect must always prevail. Resentment and grudges accomplish absolutely nothing. Be in a respectful space with total conviction and pride. It's not a concession; you aren't admitting anyone is right or wrong. If the other party unleashes vitriol, change the subject or end the conversation. It doesn't pay to fight back.
Always try to follow my mantra: *keep yourself classy and sassy!*

By contrast, if Heidi's parents were to try to dissuade her from getting married, pass judgment, or display any other kind of negative reaction, Heidi would then be well within her rights to gracefully end the conversation with total peace of mind. She doesn't have to continue the dialogue or argue her case—nor should she, as that would take them all back to square one, because at that point they already have made their positions clear. Meanwhile, Heidi has respected herself and her parents and can feel good about it, no matter the outcome. In doing so, she can hold her head high about the way she handled herself.

For many people, bad blood among family members is what causes low self-esteem. Children end up feeling guilty, as if nothing they do will ever please their parents. Meanwhile, the parents feel like failures, after having worked so hard for years to raise and educate their children, only to be treated disrespectfully. Goodwill, grace, and glory are the only ways to get past the hurdles and grant everyone a chance to be their best selves. Disrespecting someone's beliefs and values diminishes one's love for that individual and vice versa, which can be extremely difficult to repair and restore.

Personal Boundaries Command Respect

You must put in place certain boundaries to protect your self-esteem and ensure that everyone treats you with the respect you deserve. If you don't establish boundaries, others might erroneously presume one or more of the following things about you:

1. You don't have any boundaries.
2. You don't care how people treat you.
3. You can be the butt of their jokes.
4. You are insecure.
5. You can be stepped on.
6. You are a pushover who won't stand up for yourself.
7. You are someone who likes to live on the edge and welcomes boundary encroachments.

However, no one deserves disrespect or physical or emotional harm even if boundaries *haven't* been established. Being disrespectful and treating another person poorly is never acceptable. The information I present about boundaries is intended to help you protect yourself and, hopefully, avoid such challenging situations in the first place.

In any case, you never want anyone to get the (wrong) impression that you are anything other than a strong, confident person who commands and deserves respect at all times. You can be a good-natured person and still insist upon boundaries. I could offer an infinite number of examples, but the following ones should give you a clear idea of what I mean:

- Insisting that you will go only as far as kissing on the first date.
- Sharing an important piece of company information with a colleague but not allowing her access to your computer files.
- Loaning a sweater to a roommate but not permitting her to take one from your drawer at will.
- Placing your snacks in the refrigerator with the understanding that no one else can have them without your permission.
- Informing your neighbor that his dog can't poop on your lawn.
- Expressing your displeasure when someone pokes fun at the shape of your nose.
- Making it clear that you prefer to keep your private life separate from your work life.
- Telling someone who borrows something of yours that he must replace or pay for it if he loses or breaks it.
- Stressing that you will not tolerate undergarments being left on the living room floor.
- Voicing your disgust when someone intentionally belches at the dinner table and asking for it to stop.

Once a boundary has been effectively established and communicated, you have carved a line in the pavement that others cannot be allowed to pass. If someone does violate one such boundary, you have every right to feel disrespected and to do something about it. Always keep in mind that, as the recipient of the behavior, you are not at fault and should not be held accountable in any way. In fact, it's quite the opposite; the person who disrespected you should feel embarrassed and/or ashamed.

Clar-ion Call

There are degrees when it comes to when and how far you need to address a boundary violation, and it is not possible for me to cover all bases in this regard. For minor incursions when your life is not in danger, a private and honest conversation might do the trick the first time it occurs. You might begin by saying, "Hey, I'd like to discuss something with you, if you don't mind."

If, however, it's of a more serious nature—that is, physical or sexual harm—the stakes are significantly higher, and you need to report the matter to the authorities. In a workplace, anyone who breaks the company policies must be confidentially reported to the human resources department. Never feel like a "snitch" when you are protecting your boundaries, the law, and company policies.

There is some gray area with regard to when an issue needs to be taken that far, but the rule of thumb is this: if you feel hurt, threatened, or uncomfortable in any way—especially if it is a repeat offense—and are unable to address the issue directly with the person, discuss it with your coach or a trusted friend. Always seek good counsel before allowing any boundary to be crossed more than once!

You must always stand up and defend yourself when one of your boundaries has been attacked. It may feel uncomfortable and nerve wracking to bring such an issue to a person's attention or up the chain of command, but it must be done or else your self-esteem will suffer. The alternative—doing nothing—is a signal to the offender that you are fair game, and he or she thinks it's acceptable to repeat the offense.

Listen to Your Inner Voice

There are times when the available facts don't automatically signal the best decision to make regarding boundary protection. For example, let's say a woman at a bar with her friends is deliberating about whether or not she should have another drink. On one hand, she has to make an important presentation at work early the following morning. On the flip side, her friends keep telling her things like, "Oh, come on, one drink won't hurt!" and "It's so early, don't be a spoilsport!" Both perspectives seem to carry equal weight in her mind, and she can't make a decision. But then, a little voice in her head whispers, "Don't do it. Your future depends on giving an amazing presentation tomorrow. Don't take any chances that another drink might make you groggy and perform at less than your best."

Clarissa's Corner

Although you should never be afraid to say "no," you should also always stick to your guns and express yourself when you mean to say "yes"—especially when you are going up against the crowd.

Workplaces are notorious for pressuring people to agree with a majority, no matter which side you may be on (yea or nay). Some people say "no" to every idea proposed other than their own. It doesn't make them right, even if they have decision-making power or the ability to sway an entire room to their side.

Always respond with whatever response you truly believe in, even if it goes against the grain and may invite some derision. If you believe you have a great idea and the ammunition to support your position, don't hold back—no matter how much you fear being struck down. First of all, you don't know the outcome before you have tested the waters. Second, you will feel better about yourself for having thrown yourself out there. Third, you will garner respect for being brave enough to vocalize your thoughts. The worst feeling of all is the regret of not having had the courage to speak up in the first place.

Call the little voice what you will: your conscience, your intuition, your instincts, or simply your rational brain guiding you on the right path. Guess what? That little voice knows better than the 50 percent of your brain that's urging you to order another drink—and it is certainly wiser than the friends around you. You must always listen to your inner voice, even if it means disappointing your friends. When you announce to the entire table "Sorry, guys, I'd love to stay and have another drink, but I really have to go," your next step should be to throw on your coat and hat and leave. Don't wait around for them to coax you into changing your mind or start jeering at you. If you pack up and make an exit, they will admire you, respect you, and take you seriously the next time you are in a similar situation. Best of all, you will feel good about standing up against the pressure, which makes you stronger and boosts your self-esteem.

Know this: each and every move you make—the way you sit, stand, walk, talk, and so forth—impacts how people interact with you and determines whether they will respect you or not.

The Respect Killers

A well-respected person has several easily identifiable traits: honesty, dependability, trustworthiness, loyalty, generosity, morality, and humility. Can you guess what else she has? High self-esteem, of course.

By the same token, a person not known for being respectful to others often does specific things that are self-destructive and that hurt others, damage reputations, and lead to low self-esteem. The good news is that these "respect killers" can be controlled and need not define you. Can you recognize some of the following traits and behaviors in yourself and/or other people you know who have low self-esteem?

- *People pleasing*: There is nothing wrong with helping people—in fact, giving back is vital to strong self-esteem, as we discover in the next chapter. However, when a person does *everything* for other people instead of taking care of herself, it opens the door for others to take advantage. When this occurs, respect is diminished—not gained. One can always say "no" to a request.
- *Self-deprecation*: The ability to poke fun at oneself not only demonstrates a good sense of humor, it also signals humility and self-awareness. Taken too far, however, this can become a major problem. If one becomes too self-critical—meaning that instances occur with too much frequency or to an extreme degree—the negativity becomes a self-fulfilling prophecy, the opposite of the law of attraction mentioned in earlier chapters. At the same time, such behavior can become a turnoff, as it might bring other people down as well. Think of it this way: people want to spend time with confident, happy people, not those who beat up on

themselves. In time, people start to believe the self-deprecating propaganda and lose respect for that individual. In short: never speak badly about yourself, whether others are listening or not!

- *Insulting*: Great public speakers are well aware that they must "play to their audiences." It's no different in interpersonal relationships; you have to know the people with whom you are communicating, especially in a workplace. Although some people enjoy biting sarcasm, many others do not. They take words at face value, especially if they don't know you very well. It's great to be the class (or work) comedian, but not at the expense of hurting other people—even if it's inadvertent. Before experimenting with sarcasm, get to know the person in question first and be sure the jibe is worth the risk.

- *Intolerant*: We are all human and have our perspectives and breaking points in terms of what offends us. Prejudices and sexism, for example, are never acceptable in civilized cultures. But let's suppose you were to berate someone at work who has allergies and sneezes a lot. Or you snap at a child waiting ahead of you in a line for a roller coaster because she is laughing too loudly with her friends. Or you murmur and snarl to yourself when you can't get through a corridor because an elderly woman with a walker is blocking you. People who are brazenly intolerant of others are often viewed as bores and lose respect as a result.

- *Potty-mouthed*: This one is tricky! Studies have shown that people with a strong sense of humor and/or who use profanity tend to be highly intelligent. It stands to reason that this skill also helps their popularity. That said, it doesn't excuse the use of foul language in situations in which someone may become offended and/or when you don't know your audience. It's fine to be yourself with friends and family who are accustomed to what comes out of your mouth, but exercise caution when you are with strangers—especially when conversing with coworkers, clients, and customers at work. This goes for emails and texts, too, where one inappropriate word or emoji can be passed along from one person to the next indefinitely.

- *Abusive*: Any kind of abusive behavior—verbal or physical—is a big no-no, whether it's done intentionally or not. Damaging someone's property or possessions also counts as abusive. It goes without saying this is an area in which you don't want to take any risks. Respect other people and they will respect you in turn.

- *Oversharing*: Although you want to come across as an open, honest person, you also don't want to reveal too much about yourself to colleagues, clients, and customers at work—and certainly not to strangers. Personal details, such as your medical history, relationships, financial situations, and the like are all best kept private. Oversharing can make certain people uncomfortable, and it opens the door for them to make assumptions and judge you. When in doubt, be social, polite, friendly, and a good listener and you will earn the respect of others. If someone asks a question that is too personal, simply say, "I'm sorry, I'd rather not discuss that." Do not give a long-winded explanation, as that will make the other person even more curious, and rumors might start to circulate.

The upshot is this: if you are ever in doubt about how to react to something, use common sense and put yourself in the shoes of the other person. How would you respond to x and y behaviors if someone were to do them to you? Would you be offended, get angry, and/or hold a grudge? If there is even a hint this may be the case, backtrack and rethink how to approach someone who treats you that way.

Finally, remember this: *respect* is a two-way street and a powerful tool for building self-esteem, whereas *disrespect* is an absolute dead end.

Affirmation: I Respect

I respect the rights, beliefs, and values of others.
I respect the boundaries I have set for myself and hold them dear.
I respect the boundaries others have set for themselves and hold them dear.
I will garner respect from others by protecting my boundaries when needed.
I accept that some of my relationships may shift—and perhaps even end—
in my efforts to safeguard my boundaries.
If any relationships end as a result of my efforts to defend my boundaries,
I will wish those individuals well on their journeys.

REview

- Be respectful to other people, even when you disagree with them.
- Allow others sufficient time to process your point of view.
- Establish, communicate, and protect your personal boundaries at all times.
- Listen to your inner voice and do not allow other people to convince you to do things you don't want to do.
- Avoid the respect killers: negative traits and behaviors that may hurt you and/or others and can ultimately damage your reputation and reduce your self-confidence.

CHAPTER TWELVE

~

REciprocal

You're only as beautiful as your last good deed.

—Clarissa Burt, author

Pat—a beautiful and talented woman in her early thirties—was in dire straits when I first met her. She was suffering from a disease that only had a 50 percent survival rate. In addition to enduring physical pain, she experienced a host of repercussions: she had to resign from her high-paying job to take care of her health; she struggled financially; and she lost her boyfriend of many years, as he could no longer deal with the strain of supporting a woman who required so much care and attention.

Several friends and I helped Pat stay on her feet as much as we could— especially in terms of life coaching and maintaining her self-esteem—but she did all of the hard work herself by following the regime. Most importantly, she created her own purpose, mission, and vision, looked at her vision board every day, and journaled religiously.

After a full year of medical procedures, medications, and a host of other treatments, Pat was told by her doctors that a miracle had occurred: her treatments had worked! She was 100 percent in the clear and on the road to a complete recovery. I couldn't be happier for her. Once again, she followed the regime—especially the tips in the rebound phase—and made her way back.

Flash forward to present: Pat is now a best-selling author, TV personality, motivational speaker, and authority on recovery. She has legions of clients, as well as social media followers. She found her true love, whom she married, and recently had her first child. Way to go, Pat!

Now we come to the hard reality: Pat is unavailable to many of the people who helped her get back on the road to recovery and become a superstar. She hasn't thanked me or the other people—not that we need it—who helped to support her through her dark period. She has changed her phone number and does not respond to emails from those who had been part of her previous life—including me. Our mutual friends feel hurt and betrayed.

We want to feel proud and happy for Pat, except she has not reciprocated with the one thing we hoped to receive: friendship. She has forgotten who she was, where she came from, and who helped get her through her anguished times.

I wish all the best for Pat, but I do fear that her failure to practice reciprocity will come back to negatively impact her in some way, shape, or form in the future.

The idea of starting one's life over after experiencing a life-threatening ordeal like Pat's can seem both exciting and overwhelming. There are intense memories involved—physical, emotional, and perhaps even spiritual—that must be carefully managed. The easy way to begin anew is to sell everything, move away, and find new friends who aren't constant reminders of the hell you went through during that time. I totally get it!

And yet this is not the right path for anyone to follow. In order to be a whole person with self-respect, it's appropriate to acknowledge the people who supported you through all of the pain and suffering and provided comfort for you when you needed it most. Not only do they deserve reciprocity, your heart and soul need to be open enough to provide it for them.

I do not consider Pat to be a bad person. My mutual friends and I are not angry, nor do we hold a grudge against her. We want only the best for her. At the same time, the way things turned out is unfortunate for all of us—Pat included. Most of all, we miss her very much and wish we could celebrate her continued success with her.

We always must remember the people at the bottom of the ladder as we climb upward, especially if they gave us a boost on one or more of the rungs. This may not seem all that appealing if those individuals become reminders of a difficult past. Some successful people may believe that the folks they left behind will become clingy and expect favors or remain friends only to have access to celebrity.

Trust me on this: such scenarios are extremely rare! For the most part, people want to remain in your circle for one reason only: they love you and want to share in your glow and congratulate you, not steal it away. No matter what, you must always give your friends a chance; don't give up on them. They stood by you, so now it's your turn. In the unlikely event they disappoint you later on, you can decide how to react at that time (which should be to forgive them and move on).

The message is clear: reciprocity fills the heart and soul with joy for both the givers and the receivers and therefore is essential to good and lasting self-esteem and a life without regret.

The Butterfly Effect

It feels good to give back to people and the community: friends, relatives, neighbors, coworkers, community members, and even total strangers. One should feel the urge to assist others, even when the individuals haven't done something for you. You should not have any expectation of being "paid back" for your time, support, or donations or it detracts from the sincerity of the effort. The idea is that the *universe* finds a way to reward you for your selfless good deeds.

The concept I'm adapting here, commonly known as the butterfly effect, suggests that even the tiniest unrelated things can impact events in a complex system. For example, imagine a butterfly flapping its wings and causing a typhoon. Is such a thing possible? In a word, *yes*: reality is fluid and there are billions of variables for every single occurrence. One small change to these variables, and events unfold in a completely different way.

Let's demonstrate this in action. As I worked on this chapter, my collaborator's beloved cat, Misty, passed away through an odd chain of events. A family member inadvertently left the front door open a crack. Another person ran a vacuum, which spooked Misty. The cat fled to the front door, where she poked her paw through the crack just enough to squeeze through and scurry outside—in the dead of a harsh New England winter. The family searched high and low for days, leaving food outside and alerting neighbors, animal rescues, and social media groups. Four days later, poor Misty was struck by a car only two blocks from her home. What a terrible tragedy!

If any one of the variables had been different, Misty *might* still be alive—if the vacuuming had been done the day before, if the door had been shut properly, if Misty had entered the road moments after that particular driver zoomed down the street, if that driver had taken a different route that day, and so on.

Dominating Your Daily Demons

If you are having even just a temporary lapse in self-esteem, there is no better way to boost yourself up than to help out someone who is in immediate need. You feel instantaneous joy and satisfaction doing something for another person. Sometimes helping someone else is even more motivating than doing something for yourself. Not only does it benefit the other person and fill you with warmth, you are distracting your mind from whatever has been bringing you down.

This sad story aside, the butterfly effect often is used to explain events that don't have an obvious cause and effect. Most of the time, we never know how one action relates to another, directly or indirectly. Whatever the case, the butterfly effect has a great deal to do with reciprocity—which can be on a positive note, of course, if certain influence is involved. When you give back to others, you truly do not know how it will impact them. For example, if you were to hand a lottery ticket to a homeless person who then wins a million dollars, guess what? His life would be forever changed!

On a more modest scale, if instead you were to feed or clothe the homeless person, lead him to shelter, or hand him a $5 bill, any one of these simple gestures could be enough impetus to help him get back on his feet. Although there is no guarantee this would happen, you have increased the odds by changing one of those variables. By providing food or money to the homeless man, you are helping him at that moment, which sustains him at least for a while and instills in you a sense of accomplishment. There is no better way to pump up your self-esteem than such a selfless, reciprocal act—giving back in equal measure the benefits that you have received from the world, not necessarily as any kind of payback to a specific individual.

Sweet Charity

There are myriad ways to be charitable. Certainly, you can donate money, food, clothing, or other items to the cause of your choice. Equally as important is volunteering your time to help in some physical fashion, such as serving food to the needy in a soup kitchen. There is no social cause that is too big or too small: everything counts, whether it's at a food bank, a homeless shelter, a city cleanup project, a school fundraiser, a community garden, or an animal rescue facility. Some people take it a step further, becoming a Big Brother or Big Sister to a child or teenager. Others may mentor adults who are struggling financially or in the job market. We all contribute as best we can in whatever manner is right for us.

Clar-ion Call

In both Judaism and Christianity, there exists a practice of donating 10 percent of one's earnings to charity. Judaism even has a name for it: *tzedakah*. (In the introduction, you'll recall I introduced a similar concept known as *tithing*.) Although your objective is to help community members in need, according to Judaic theory, you ultimately will receive double the amount you have provided to others.

You don't have to be religious to take on this noble 10 percent practice, if you have the means to do so. Nor are you obligated to give the full 10 percent. Whatever you can afford and feels right to you is perfectly acceptable.

Personally, I have served roles with a wide variety of organizations over the years and continue to do so. These are just a few: Domestic Shelters.org (spokesperson), Project C.U.R.E., Childhelp U.S.A., the

American Heart Association, the Italian Red Cross, Telefono Azurro Italy (abused children), Dress for Success, and Catwalk for a Cause. I was also blessed with the opportunity for a private audience with Pope John Paul II regarding social work efforts. I enjoy every minute of these volunteer efforts and feel renewed energy, optimism, and self-esteem after each one.

The Golden Rule Is Golden

Although the Golden Rule has religious roots—specifically addressed as the words of Jesus in Matthew 7:12 and Luke 6:31 and also appearing in Buddhism, Judaism, Islam, Taoism, and other religions in various forms—you do not have to believe in a particular religion to abide by it. In fact, you don't have to be devout at all! Being a kind and good person is an expectation of every human being at all times.

Essentially, the Golden Rule goes like this: *do unto others as you would have them do unto you.* I've mentioned the concept of putting yourself in other people's shoes throughout this book, which relates to empathy. The Golden Rule takes this further by including the action verb "do," which signifies that you must treat other people well because you would never want it to be otherwise for yourself. There is an action implied in the sentiment which, in my view, includes both physical and verbal action. It's obvious that a physically aggressive act, such as a slap, would be unwanted by you or anyone. The same could be said for an insult, which can cause emotional pain. Taken even further, this idea extends to hurting the loved ones of other people, their property, and their pets, too.

Even More Reasons to Help Others

There are so many more reasons for being charitable that I could fill an entire book on the subject. I have seen firsthand how charitable adults become role models for their kids, as well as for the parents and children of others. The goodwill becomes contagious from one family to another and from one community to the next. When people act with reciprocity, they tend to spread goodwill throughout the surrounding area, and people become kinder and more generous overall. To be sure, when people witness you performing generous acts, they will have renewed respect for you, which, as we know from the previous chapter, provides bountiful self-esteem.

Clarissa's Corner

Some people find it challenging enough to balance their own accounts and therefore don't feel they have enough money for themselves, much less to donate to charity.

Au contraire! The amount you give doesn't matter in the least—as long as you give *something*. Some people keep jars in the kitchen full of spare coins. Every time a family member has change in his or her pockets, the money goes right into the jar. Found money—such as on the ground or in the pocket of an old jacket—can go in there as well. For some, the charity container pulls double duty as a "swear jar," in which money is paid every time a curse word is uttered. Imagine how quickly this would add up in the average household!

Charity fundraising ideas are limited only by the imagination. You could have a garage sale or bake sale and donate a percentage of the proceeds to charity. Or, you could simply convert the five cents you would receive from returning recyclable cans and bottles into charitable donations.

Give the gift of giving!

As if all of that isn't enough, here are some additional reasons why donating money or volunteering is beneficial.

1. *Health benefits.* A survey by the National Institutes of Health found that people who donated just a small amount of money had heightened amounts of dopamine—the neurotransmitter in the human body—which stimulated the pleasure centers in the brain. This also occurs when eating chocolate or while making love. That sounds plenty worth it to me!

2. *Tax rewards.* This shouldn't be a reason to encourage charity and volunteerism, but I'll take the favorable result however I can get it. Yes, in the United States and other countries, you can write

off approved donations on your tax returns. Check with your accountant or the IRS website to verify the latest information about deductions.

3. *Better money management.* Donating on a regular basis—such as monthly—provides a reminder to check on your financial status each time. Looking at your accounts from an entirely different perspective—"How much can I afford to give this month?"—ensures that you stay on top of your bills, debt, and savings while simultaneously helping others.

4. *You never know what will happen.* Going back to the butterfly effect: you never know whom you may meet while volunteering your time at a soup kitchen, church, synagogue, or anywhere else. Perhaps someone working right beside you is the CEO of a major corporation and is so impressed by your efforts to help others that she hires you for a position in her company. Or perhaps a struggling person whom you assist—or maybe her offspring—goes on to achieve greatness after your kindness inspired her to try something different. One thing we do know: lack of involvement has zero impact on everyone, including on you and your self-esteem.

Community and Country

You might be thinking the expression "for the greater good" has connotations of conformity or perhaps even a cult. For me, the greater good means being part of something much bigger than myself: serving community and country.

Friendly Neighbors

There are a few basic things you can do to be a solid citizen: taking care of your property and respecting that of others; offering assistance to neighbors when called upon (shoveling an elderly neighbor's snow, for example); cleaning up after your pet if you have one; and keeping an eye on your neighbors' homes when you know they are away.

You don't want to be one of those stereotypical nosy neighbors from old TV sitcoms (such as Gladys Kravitz on *Bewitched*). However, you do want to know who your neighbors are in order to be able to identify them from potentially threatening people. A friendly smile, wave, and "hello" when passing them by is always welcome. In this way, your neighbors also will feel more comfortable being there for you if you ever require assistance.

Solid Citizens

It doesn't matter what your political affiliation, ethnicity, religion, or favorite football team. In the end, we are all part of one nation—whether the United States or another country—and we all breathe the same air and drink the same water. National pride can help you to feel part of something bigger, which means increased pride, strength, and self-esteem.

There are simple things we can do as solid citizens, including:

- Voting.
- Celebrating in parades.
- Honoring veterans.
- Serving jury duty.
- Supporting national parks and monuments.
- Being tolerant of everyone's beliefs.
- Displaying a flag.
- Joining a town council or chamber of commerce.
- Becoming involved in community programs.
- Organizing a block party with your neighbors.
- Obeying the laws.
- Respecting authority, such as police.
- Contributing to local firehouses.
- Cooperating when the city, state, or national government needs your help.

Every effort counts when it comes to improving the quality of life for yourself and others. As stated in the last chapter, put yourself in the shoes of others and be mindful of the feelings of others at all times.

Clarissa's Corner

Whether you are aware of it or not, there exists a National Association for Self-Esteem. Its purpose "is to fully integrate self-esteem into the fabric of American society so that every individual, no matter what their age and background, experiences personal worth and happiness." The website, https://healthyselfesteem.org, offers a "Self-Guided Tour" to rate your self-esteem, as well as lessons and activities.

Other organizations include:

- The Dove Self-Esteem Project: www.dove.com/us/en/dove -self-esteem-project.html
- I am B.E.A.U.T.I.F.U.L. (Brave, Energetic, Assertive, Unique, Tenacious, Important, Fabulous, Unequaled, Loved): www .iambeautiful.org
- The Love Yourself Project: www.loveyourselfproject.org /ourstory.php
- The Hope for Healing Foundation: https://hopeforhealing-foundation.org/you-are-good-enough/?gclid=Cj0KCQiA6t6A BhDMARIsAONIYyz7PcPpOBuQsbJCccnMF76nym6EKyG 5sRKXUJ-oGGTpVchm-3mGTHcaAizlEALw_wcB

Check them out!

One more important reminder: since you are now at the end of your journey through the regime, it is important for you to take a good look at your vision board. Is it all about you? Are your loved ones, neighbors, community members, and colleagues at work part of your vision board in some way? If not, what graphic can you now add to it to embed them in the assemblage of images? It is then—and only then—that you can feel whole, brim with self-esteem, and truly be the person you were meant to be.

Affirmation: I Will Be Generous

I will donate my time and money to good causes to open my heart and soul to others.

I will be financially generous to others as much as I can afford.
I will find creative ways to serve my fellow community members.
I will share the benefits of my charitable efforts with others to encourage
them to do the same.
I will be a kind person, even to those who offend or hurt me.
I will become stronger each time I do a kind act for others.
I will not judge others who do not feel they are able to donate to charity or
volunteer.
I will not expect any reciprocity from the individuals who receive my donations.
I will honor my community and country.

REview

- Become especially thankful for and generous to loyal and supportive friends, family, and neighbors when you meet with success.
- Recognize that every action has a butterfly effect upon something else, whether it is tangible or not.
- Consider making a donation or volunteering to your charity of choice.
- Incentivize reciprocal actions by understanding the potential benefits of helping others.
- Devote thought, time, and attention to being a good neighbor and upright citizen at all times.
- Congratulate yourself for completing the regime!

~

Final Clar-ion Call

My Dearest REgimers,

Thank you for staying the course! Having followed the *RE* plan mapped out in this book, you are well on your way to becoming the person you are meant to be. Do it now and continuously with vigor! The resulting positive impact on your life and the lives of those around you is the universe's best work—so have fun being the best you!

As you probably realize, there are literally *thousands* of *RE* words that could have been selected and featured in this book. I did my best to narrow them down to the most universal dozen that would serve the greatest impact as part of the regimen. If you wish to take it further, here are several other *RE* words to consider as extra credit that can also boost your self-esteem:

- *REcipes*: Pull out a cookbook and try preparing a few new dishes. Cooking and baking are fun activities for boosting self-esteem and taking your mind off of life's problems.
- *REcondition*: Throughout the regime, I presented ideas for improving the start of your day, such as waking up an hour earlier in order to be more productive. You can also recondition your outlook as you rise by the way in which you greet the new day.

When you first wake up, sit up, touch your feet to the floor, and say "thank you" for another day. In doing so, you set a positive vibration and intention for how things play out during the course of your daily activities. You become a partner in co-creating the kind of day you want to have, rather than passively allowing life to happen to you.

- *REcognition*: Carefully walk the fine line between conceit and confidence. Someone who is full of herself puts people off, rather than drawing them in. However, the right amount of confidence in who you are will draw people in. Generally speaking, toot your horn primarily when you need to show your supervisors at work that you have what it takes. When in social situations, the less self-praise, the better. In fact, rather than boasting about yourself, compliment others. Their reactions will make you feel better than if you had been speaking about yourself.

- *REkindle*: I'm not referring to romantic relationships. Which old friendships have faded over the years but are worth reviving?

- *REdiscover*: What childhood passions and hobbies have you forgotten but would love to try again? If you painted pictures when you were young, what is stopping you from picking up a sketchpad and pencil or an easel and paintbrush right now?

- *REtry*: Along the lines of *rediscover*, what were some things you were *not* successful at when you were younger that you would like another chance to conquer? Now is the time to start all over again with another effort. Why not? You have the benefit of knowledge and experience that you did not have back then.

What *RE* words can you add to the dozen and a half that I've presented in this book? Do not feel limited! In fact, give some new ones a try and then write to me at Clarissa@clarissaburt.com to let me know how they worked out for you.

It is my sincere hope that *The Self-Esteem REgime* has helped you reverse and shed negativity in your life, whether caused by voices deep inside or by external forces. Be mindful that it is easy to relapse due to circumstances that arise, so keep this book right by your side and refer to it often.

The tips and advice I've offered have been written to stand the test of time, and you can always flip back to any specific chapter. Please be diligent about writing in your journal, looking at your vision board, and updating progress on your goals!

Remember: you have the power to enhance your life, as well as the lives of those around you. Your positive impact on others is your legacy. You write the story—make it a good one!

My greatest hope is for you to live the life you desire with ease, joy, and glory. Living a happy, fulfilled, and esteemed life is your birthright. Your dreams are unique to you, and you deserve to feel happy and fulfilled. If you're waiting for a sign, this is it!

Finally, always keep it classy and sassy, and do your best to breathe rare air.

With esteem and good wishes,

Clarissa Burt
April 2021

~

Additional Powerful Tools

Whenever you are struggling with your confidence, I suggest you try reciting the following: the Optimist's Creed, the Awakening Affirmation, the Evening Affirmation, and the Blessing for My Body. These are powerful tools to keep you motivated, confident, and on track.

It is perfectly fine to tailor these affirmations to fit your needs and adapt to specific situations, as long as they do not focus on "mistakes" or slip into negative thoughts.

The Optimist's Creed

Promise yourself . . .
to be so strong that nothing can disturb your peace of mind.
to speak health, happiness, and prosperity to every person you meet.
to make all of your friends and loved ones feel that there is something wonderful in them.
to look at the sunny side of everything and make your optimistic thoughts come true.
to think favorable thoughts of others.
to accomplish all of your goals.
to fulfill your mission, vision, and purpose.
to dream of only the best, to think of only the best, to believe only the best, to work only for the best, and to expect only the best.

The Awakening Affirmation

I call forth all of the forces of love and healing that I might experience a pronounced shift in my healing process.
I ask that this healing begin immediately.
I am ready to be cleansed, purified, and raised up to my highest level of being.
I do not know what this miracle will look like, and I release the need to oversee each and every detail.
Here and now: I make myself available to the awakening and all of the enlightening possibilities each day brings.
May my awakening light up the entire world.
And so it will be for this day until I return peacefully this evening.

The Evening Affirmation

Today . . .
I have done my best to accomplish my daily goals.
I have worked toward fulfilling my mission, purpose, and vision.
I have sought to control only what I am able to control.
I have treated myself and others with respect.
I have been honest in all of my dealings.
I have loved with all of my heart.
I have done everything possible to improve the world.
I have only thought and spoken positive words about myself and others.

The Blessing for My Body

I would like to thank . . .
my eyes, for looking, seeing, taking in, regarding, and closing when needed to shield me from pain.
my hair, for protecting, covering, and adding grace and beauty.
my nails, for guarding and serving as windows for my fingertips.
my brain, for providing images, thoughts, knowledge, and invention and for serving as a channel and switchboard.
my ears, for hearing, listening, and acknowledging sounds.
my jaw, for offering firmness, smiling, and chewing.
my tongue, for tasting, language, flexibility, and fluidity.
my lips, for stretching and giving softness and tenderness.
my teeth, for biting and enabling sustenance to enter my body.

my face, for facing the world and for providing my countenance and expressions to the world.

my eyebrows, for shielding.

my nose, for filtering, guiding, and inhaling the wonders of the earth.

my skin, for covering, protecting, and feeling.

my fingers, hands, and arms, for grasping, reaching, and embracing.

my neck, for upholding and directing.

my shoulders, for framing.

my elbows, for flexing.

my legs, for standing tall and taking me wherever I need to go.

my knees, for bending.

my feet, for holding my weight and balancing me.

my ankles, for granting mobility.

my heels, for digging in.

my toes, for balancing.

my thighs and buttocks, for giving me strength and power.

my spine, for holding me upright.

my stomach, for digesting food and sending nutrients throughout my body.

my breasts, for nurturing.

my heart, for loving.

my lungs, for breathing in the air of life.

my blood, for serving as the fluid of my being.

my spirit, for providing vision and purpose.

Thank you, my beautiful body, which performs all of these wonders and so much more.

APPENDIX B

REsources

Chapter Sources

Chapter 4

National Children's Alliance. "National Statistics on Child Abuse." www
.nationalchildrensalliance.org/media-room/national-statistics-on-child
-abuse/#:~:text=In%20substantiated%20child%20abuse%20cases,were%20
victimized%20by%20a%20parent.&text=Child%2Don%2Dchild%20
abuse%20is,of%20the%20total%20were%20teenagers.

Statista. "Violent Crime Statistics in the U.S." www.statista.com/topics/1750
/violent-crime-in-the-us/.

NCADV. "Statistics." https://ncadv.org/STATISTICS.

Aldridge, Kristen. "Hollywood's Most Improved Awards." *Shape*, March 2013.
www.shape.com/celebrities/celebrity-photos/hollywoods-most-improved
-awards?slide=939cdfd4-19f8-4980-9ce3-f513502014ba#939cdfd4-19f8
-4980-9ce3-f513502014ba.

Hay, Louise. "What Is Mirror Work?" www.louisehay.com/what-is-mirror-work/.

Chapter 5

LaBonta, Lo'eau. "Human Energy Converted to Electricity." Stanford University Coursework, December 6, 2014. http://large.stanford.edu/courses/2014
/ph240/labonta1/#:~:text=The%20average%20human%2C%20at%20
rest,can%20output%20over%202%2C000%20watts.

Donne, John. "No Man Is an Island." https://web.cs.dal.ca/~johnston/poetry/island.html.

Chapter 6
Murray, Rheana. "British *Vogue* Features 100-Year-Old Model Bo Gilbert in Centennial Issue." Today.com, May 2, 2016. www.today.com/style/british-vogue-features-100-year-old-model-bo-gilbert-centennial-t90066

Chapter 7
Foster, Dawn. "How Being Poor Can Lead to a Negative Spiral of Fear and Self-loathing." Guardian.com, June 30, 2015. www.theguardian.com/society/2015/jun/30/poverty-negative-spiral-fear-self-loathing.

Chapter 8
Healthline.com. "Protein Intake—How Much Protein Should You Eat Per Day?" www.healthline.com/nutrition/how-much-protein-per-day.
CDC.gov. "Only 1 in 10 Adults Get Enough Fruits or Vegetables." www.cdc.gov/media/releases/2017/p1116-fruit-vegetable-consumption.html
Mayo Clinic Staff. "Water: How Much Should You Drink Every Day?" www.mayoclinic.org/healthy-lifestyle/nutrition-and-healthy-eating/in-depth/water/art-20044256.

Chapter 12
Levy, Jessica (for Angel View). "The Science behind Why Giving to Charity Feels So Good." DessertSun.com, December 2018. www.desertsun.com/story/sponsor-story/angel-view/2018/12/07/science-behind-why-giving-charity-feels-so-good/2232037002/.

Recommended Books

Anthony, Robert. *The Ultimate Secrets of Total Self-Confidence.* Berkley: paperback, 2008.
Aron, Elaine N. *The Highly Sensitive Person: How to Thrive When the World Overwhelms You.* Broadway: paperback, 1997.
Bowen, Will. *A Complaint Free World: How to Stop Complaining and Start Enjoying the Life You Always Wanted.* Harmony: paperback, 2013.
Brown, Brené. *The Gifts of Imperfection: Let Go of Who You Think You're Supposed to Be and Embrace Who You Are.* Hazeldon: paperback, 2010.

Carter, David Bonham. *A Practical Guide to Building Self-Esteem: Accept, Value and Empower Yourself.* Icon, paperback, 2019.

Fannin, Jeffrey L. *Commanding the Power of Thought: Volume I.* Self-published: paperback, 2020.

———. *Commanding the Power of Thought: Volume II.* Self-published: paperback, 2020.

Gay, Nora Almamia. *Get Minted! Learn to Build Massive Wealth in the Midst of Uncertainties.* Nora Gay: paperback, 2020.

Gershon, David, and Gale Straub. *Empowerment: The Art of Creating Your Life as You Want It.* Sterling Ethos: paperback, 2011.

Goldsmith, Barton. *100 Ways to Boost Your Self-Confidence: Believe in Yourself and Others Will Too.* Weiser: paperback, 2010.

Goleman, Daniel. *Working with Emotional Intelligence.* Bantam: hardcover, 1998.

Hay, Louise. *Mirror Work: 21 Days to Heal Your Life.* Hay House: paperback, 2016.

Hill, Napoleon. *Think and Grow Rich.* Sound Wisdom: paperback, 2016.

Kaiser, Shannon. *The Self-Love Experiment.* TarcherPerigee: paperback, 2017.

Lechter, Sharon. *Think and Grow Rich for Women: Using Your Power to Create Success and Significance.* Tarcher/Perigee: paperback, 2015.

Miller, MPP, Caroline Adams, and Michael B. Frisch. *Creating Your Best Life: The Ultimate Life List Guide.* Sterling: paperback, 2011.

Mongelluzzo, Nanette Burton. *The Everything Guide to Self-Esteem.* Adams Media: paperback, 2011.

Murphy, Joseph. *The Power of the Subconscious Mind.* St. Martin's Essentials: paperback, 2019.

Perera, Karl. *Self-Esteem Secrets: 12 Steps to Success.* CreateSpace: paperback, 2012.

Saban, Cheryl. *What Is Your Self-Worth? A Woman's Guide to Validation.* Hay House: paperback, 2010.

Sweeney, Patrick. *Fear Is Fuel: The Surprising Power to Help You Find Purpose, Passion, and Performance.* Rowman & Littlefield: hardcover, 2020.

Index

173

~

About the Authors

Clarissa Burt is an award-winning actress, international media personality, producer, director, writer, author, motivational speaker, and supermodel. Her brainchild, *In the Limelight*, is an online multimedia portal comprised of video, a podcast, and a digital magazine dedicated to offering educational, empowering, and entertaining subject matter. *In the Limelight* is a quarterly digital publication that may be found on PressReader.com and ClarissaBurt.com.

At eighteen, Clarissa signed with the Wilhelmina Modeling Agency in Manhattan. Soon after, she moved to Milan, where she began appearing on hundreds of magazine covers, such as *Harper's Bazaar*, *Vogue*, and *Cosmopolitan*. She became known as one of the top thirty runway models in the world in the 1980s, gracing important designer catwalks in Milan, Rome, Paris, New York, and Japan. She modeled for global cosmetic houses, such as Revlon and Dior Helena Rubenstein, and was chosen as "the face" for Orlane Cosmetics for a decade.

Clarissa's extensive international social work garnered her two private audiences with Pope John Paul II. As a women's advocate and a leader of social change for a new standard of living, she was instrumental as ambassador to the United States for the Walking Africa campaign that awarded African women the Nobel Peace Prize in 2011. Clarissa is the first American to present at the Kremlin and appear on the front page of a Russian newspaper. In February 2018, she was awarded the Certificate of Global Honor by the University of Pune, India. In December of that year, she was awarded the Women of Excellence Award by the Women's Economic Forum.

As an actress, Clarissa's films include *The NeverEnding Story II* (portraying the mean queen Xayide) and the Italian production *Caruso Pascosky di Padre Polacco* (playing Giulia). She appeared in hundreds of Italian television shows, becoming a household name in that country.

Clarissa has also been a television and film producer. Clarissa Burt Media Group, founded in Italy, began with productions that included the nationally broadcast three-hour live broadcast of the Miss Universe Pageant, the World Sports Awards, Quizzauto, and *Behind the Scenes with the Miss*—all garnering her various coveted media awards internationally. In 2019 she was associate producer for the film *Wish Man*.

Her prior books include *The Italian Gluten-Free Gastronomy Cookbook: The Art of Preparing and Savoring Gluten-Free* and contributions to *The Rise*, *Off the Coast of Zanzibar*, and *Stickability* (by Greg S. Reid).

Among her numerous charitable efforts and honorable mentions: honorary member American Chamber of Commerce in Italy; honorary member Italy-USA Foundation; honorary member Rotary Club International Rome; U.S. Ambassador Noble Peace Prize for African Women; Who's Who of American Women; Who's Who of International Women; City Council Woman Ardea Rome; Candidate for European Parliament; spokesperson Telefono Azzurro—Abused Children; spokesperson International Red Cross; and spokesperson National Prevention Day appointed by Silvio Berlusconi, Prime Minister of Italy. Her social media pages may be found here:

Facebook	www.facebook.com/ClarissaBurtOfficial
LinkedIn	http://linkedin.com/in/clarissaburt
Twitter	www.twitter.com/clarissaburt
Pinterest	http://pinterest.com/clarissaburt
Instagram	http://instagram.com/clarissaburt
Tumblr	http://clarissaburt.tumblr.com
Website	www.clarissaburt.com

Clarissa Burt resides in the Phoenix, Arizona, area.

Award-winning writer, novelist, screenwriter, literary agent, and former book publisher **Gary M. Krebs** is the founder of GMK Writing and Editing, Inc. He received his BFA from the Dramatic Writing Program, Tisch School of the Arts (New York University).

Before writing full time and launching his own business, he was associate publisher at Brilliance Publishing (a division of Amazon Publishing); vice president, group publisher, McGraw-Hill Professional; group publisher, Globe Pequot Press; publisher, Adams Media (a division of F+W Publications); publishing director, Rodale; and publishing director, Macmillan Publishing. Prior to serving as publisher, he was an acquisitions editor at several houses and U.S. editor of *The Guinness Book of Records.*

His novel, *Little Miss of Darke County: The Origins of Annie Oakley,* was published to great acclaim in 2020 and has been optioned in Hollywood as a feature film. His other credited writings include *Playing Dead* (by Monique Faison Ross), *Wealth Made Easy* (Dr. Greg S. Reid with Gary M. Krebs), *Creating Sales Stars* (Stephan Schiffman with Gary M. Krebs), *The Rock and Roll Reader's Guide,* and *The Guinness Book of Sports Records.*

Gary lives in Fairfield, Connecticut. His website may be found here: www.gmkwritingandediting.com. His Huffington Post blog may be found here: www.huffingtonpost.com/author/gary-m-krebs.